よい「意思決定」ができるパターン ... 55
「年老いた自分」と会話する ... 56
スパッとタバコをやめられる方法 ... 59
将来を「見る体験」が自分を変える ... 61

第4章 あなたは「ミラーニューロン」に動かされている

「他人の行動」を変える方法 ... 66
「自己」の認識には「好きな人」も入っている ... 68
無意識に影響を受けてしまう ... 71
「思い浮かべる」だけで意志力が強くなる ... 73
「拷問テスト」とは何か？ ... 75

なぜ、2時間「ストップ」を繰り返す
脳に「欲求」と「行動」をつなげさせない

第5章 私がいちばん使っている方法

欲求を静かに見つめる
失敗を気にすればするほど意志力は下がる
「自分と対話する」ための戦略
よい自分になるための「5つの考え方」
「自分の知らない自分」を見つける
「悩むこと」「苦しむこと」は当たり前

77 79 81　86 88 89 93 95 97

第6章 日本のみなさんの疑問に答えます

上手に「ものの見方を変える」にはどうすればいいですか？ ... 100

「科学」によって意志力の「何」がわかりましたか？ ... 103

脳科学を「ビジネスに生かす」にはどうすればいいですか？ ... 106

「将来の自分」をイメージする方法を教えてください ... 108

English Transcript ... I

第 1 章

「難しいこと」を
実行する力をつける

「あなたの問題」から考えはじめよう

こんにちは。

みなさんにお会いできて光栄です。

講演にお越しくださって、ありがとうございます。

今回初めての来日となり、おかげさまで大変楽しくすごしています。いろいろな誘惑に出会いますが、意志力を発揮して打ち勝っています。それにしてもたくさんの方々にお集まりいただき、感謝申し上げます。

本日の講演がみなさんのお役に立つものとなれば幸いです。

では早速、みなさんに質問をしたいと思います。

意志力について講演を行なうときは、たいていこの質問から始めるんです。世界中どこへ行っても、私はこうお訊きします。

第1章
「難しいこと」を実行する力をつける

「意志力の問題であなたが手を焼いているのはどんなことですか？」
意志力や自制心の問題で、あなたにとって最大のチャレンジはどんなことでしょうか？

驚いたことに、世界中どこの国へ行っても、多くの人が同じような問題を抱えているようなのです。

今回私は初めて日本へやって来ましたので、日本の現実を知るためにも、ここに挙げた例は日本のみなさんにとってもおなじみの問題かどうか、なかには手を焼いているものもあるかどうか、お訊きしてみたいと思ったのです。

まず、多くの人が挙げるのが、食べ物をはじめとする好物に感じる誘惑です。好物を目の前にすると、誘惑に負けてしまおうか、それとも我慢しようか、心のなかで葛藤が生まれます。みなさんにもそんな経験はありますか？　おひとり手が挙がりましたね。よかったです、アメリカ人だけではないとわかってほっとしました。

それから、時間の使い方が下手だという悩みもよく聞きます。大事な目標があるのでがんばろうと思っているとします。けれども、そういう長期的な目標の達成には役に立たなくても、目先のことだけ考えれば、もっと面白くて楽しいことはほかにいくらでもあるので、ついそういうことに時間を使ってしまいがちなのです。

トランプを重ねて橋をつくるのに夢中になったり、テクノロジーやテレビゲームにはまったりすると、あっという間に多くの時間が過ぎてしまいます。

「自信のないこと」をやろうとするのが難しい

意志力の問題で最も大変なのは、うまくやれるかどうか自信のないこと、不安や心配を感じることに、思い切って挑戦しようと決心することだ、という声もよ

第1章
「難しいこと」を実行する力をつける

く聞きます。

うまくいくだろうか、そもそもこれは正しい選択なのだろうか。

そんな不安や疑念を抱きながらも、思い切ってやろうと決心して実行に踏み切るには、かなりの自制心と意志力が必要です。

また、日々のストレスやトラブル、職場の人間関係などに悩まされながらも感情のバランスを保つのはなかなか大変です。

怒りや悲しみやストレスといった心のなかのさまざまな感情に向き合

い、そうした感情が自分自身や周りの人に害を及ぼさないように注意するのも大変です。

　私たちはそうやってさまざまな人間関係のなかで感情のバランスを保ち、心理的に健康な状態でいようと努力します。

　最後に、現在の楽しみを犠牲にしたくはないけれど、将来のためになることもしたい、という悩みもよく聞きます。将来のためにはならないような目先の快楽を優先するか、それとも我慢して将来の幸せのためにがんばるか。私たちはよくそんな選択を迫られます。

　多くの人の話を聞いてみると、現在の自分のためになることと、将来の自分のためになることを、それぞれどのくらい行なえばよいのか、そのバランスを決めるのが難しいようです。

14

第1章
「難しいこと」を実行する力をつける

「自分を妨害する自分」と戦う

みなさんにも、それは自分にも当てはまると思うことはあったでしょうか？

もしとくに思い当たるようなことがなかったとしても、自分が困っている意志力の問題とはかけ離れた問題もあるのだな、と受けとめていただければ幸いです。

私の言う意志力というのは、たとえ自分の価値観や目標にふさわしいことを選択するのが困難に思えるときでも、あえてそのような選択をする力のことです。

あるいは、何をするのが正しいのかよくわからないときでも、将来の自分が後悔するようなことではなく、感謝したくなるようなことを選択するための賢さや強さ、判断力とも言えるでしょう。

このことは、生きていくうえで知恵や賢さや勇気を必要とする、あらゆることに当てはまります。

15

これまで多くの方がおっしゃっていたのは、前向きなことをしよう、人生に変化を起こそうと強く思っているときに、もうひとりの自分が現れて目標を妨げようとする感じがする、ということです。

ためになることをしようと思っているにもかかわらず、そうしたくないと思う自分がいるような感覚です。

まるで自分自身と戦っているような感じだと多くの人が言っています。よいと思ったことを選択するか、それとも誘惑に負けてしまうか。それは、哲学者や偉大な宗教の指導者たちが時代を超えて思索を重ねてきたことでもあります。

このような人間に共通する悩みが、現代心理学や脳の研究によって、今後さらにどれだけ解明されていくのか。私は科学者として、そのことに非常に興味をもっています。なぜ私たちは、最高の自分になって目標を達成するのをみずから妨げるような心の葛藤を、たびたび感じてしまうのでしょうか？

第1章
「難しいこと」を実行する力をつける

脳が「快楽」に負けるとき

本日お話ししたいのは、そんな心のなかのシーソーの問題です。たいていの人には覚えがあるように、私たちはよい自分になりたいと思っていても、つい誘惑に負けてしまいます。いったいどうすればよい自分になれるのでしょうか。

では、まず神経科学による最新の知見をご紹介しましょう。

なぜ私たちの心にはこれほど多くの葛藤が生じるのでしょうか——相反するふたつの自己のせめぎ合いの問題です。

これに関し、この10年で神経科学の分野から出てきた最も説得力のある考え方は、頭のなかに脳は文字通りひとつしかないけれども、むしろ脳はふたつあると考えたほうがわかりやすいというものです。

つまり、脳にはふたつのモードが存在し、それらが切り替わることによってまったく異なる自分になってしまうのです。

脳がいっぽうのモードになっているとき、人はそのモードに見合った目標を意識し、性格もそれにふさわしくなり、そのモードならではの意思決定を行ないます。

ところが、もういっぽうのモードに切り替わってしまうと、まったく別の性格が表れます。

そうすると、やろうとすることも目標もがらりと変わり、正反対の意思決定を行ないます。

一日じゅうどころか一生のあいだ、私たちの脳ではこのようにふたつのモードが切り替わります。

脳のふたつのモードのうち、ひとつはとても衝動的です。
したがって、脳がこちらのモードになっていると、私たちは目先の利益しか考

第1章
「難しいこと」を実行する力をつける

えられなくなります。手軽な快楽にしか興味がなくなり、つらいことを避けようとします。いま現在のことしか考えられなくなるのです。

しかし、脳がもうひとつのモード、つまり、「衝動的な自己」とは逆の「自己コントロール」の状態にあるときには、私たちは目先のことにとらわれず、もっと大きな視野で人生を見すえることができます。

長期的な目標を見失うことなく、いまやることが将来的にどんな影響をもたらすかについても、ちゃんとわきまえています。自分の価値観や大事だと思っていることも忘れません。

自分が他人との関わり合いのなかに存在することも理解し、ほかの人の立場からも物事を見て、自分のニーズと他人のニーズをうまく調和させることができます。

そのような状態にあるときは、時間の使い方についても、誘惑に負けるか、それとも自分にとって困難なことをあえて行なうかについても、まったく異なる選択を行ないます。つまり、脳がどちらのモードであるかによって、私たちの決断は大きく異なってくるわけです。

「大きな視野」で物事を見る力

さて、意志力には３つの力があります。

すなわち、大きな視野で物事を見て、長期的な目標を見失わずに、たとえ困難であっても、こうしておいてよかった、とあとから思えるようなことをするための力です。

いまご覧いただいているイラストは、脳のなかに存在する異なる意志力を示しています。

第 1 章
「難しいこと」を実行する力をつける

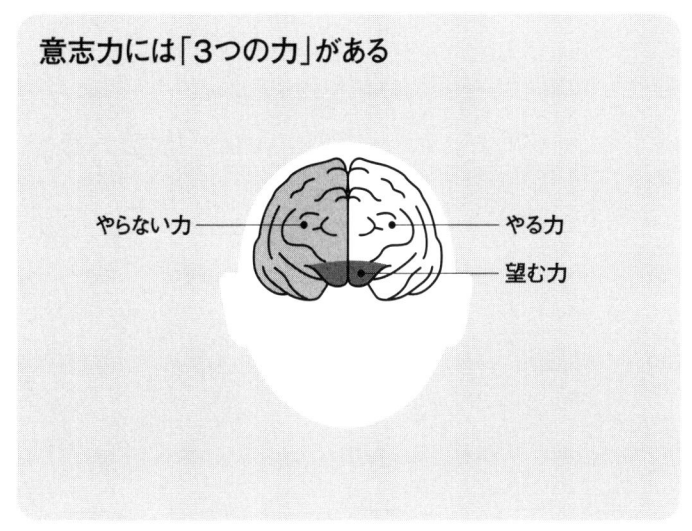

脳のこの部分には、前頭前皮質があります。

前頭前皮質の左側の部分は、困難なことを行なう力をつかさどっています。

たとえば、早起きして、勉強や運動などエネルギーや注意力の要ることを行なおうとしたり、あるいは面倒なことを先延ばしにしたくなったりしたときに、脳のこの部分が働くことによって、私たちはやる気を起こし、難しくてもやってやろう、という気になるのです。

それを「やる力」と呼びます。あ

とになって「よかった」と思えるようなことを行なう力です。

前頭前皮質の右側の部分は、誘惑に抵抗するという重要な役割をもっています。たとえ体じゅうが誘惑に負けて目の前の快楽に走ることで「イエス」と言おうとしても、脳のこの部分はきっぱりと「ノー」と言います。

これを「やらない力」と呼びます。自分自身がよくない方向に傾き、自己破壊的な行動に走りそうになったときに、「ノー」と言う力です。

3つめの力は、最もとらえどころがないかもしれません。

それは、気が散ったり、誘惑に出会ったりしても、自分が本当に望んでいることを忘れない、「望む力」です。

感情が乱れたりストレスを感じたりしたとき、つい我を忘れたり、本当に望んでいることを忘れたりせずにいられるでしょうか？

自分はどうやって世の中に貢献したいのか、どんなふうに生きていきたいのか

第 1 章
「難しいこと」を実行する力をつける

――そういうことを見失わずにいられるでしょうか？

それも誘惑に抵抗するのと同じくらい大きな力であり、スキルです。

つねに自分にとって大事な目標を忘れず、こういう人生にしたい、というビジョンをはっきりと思い描けることは、「やる力」「やらない力」に勝るとも劣らない重要なスキルであり、力であると言えます。

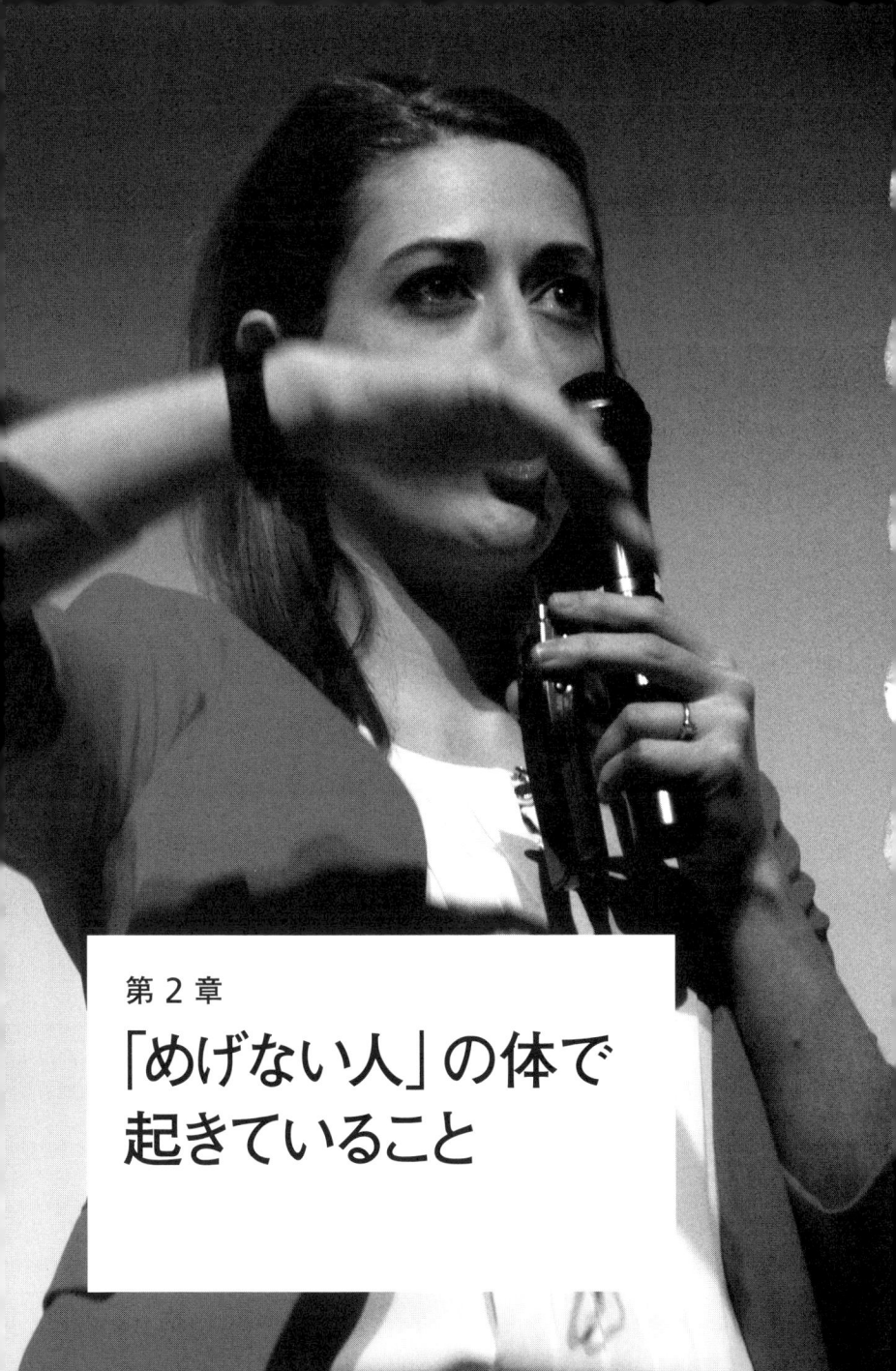

第 2 章
「めげない人」の体で
起きていること

私が最も驚いた研究

本日の講演のテーマは、どうしたらよい自分になれるかを理解することです。
どうしたら誘惑に対して「ノー」と言える賢さと勇気をもった自分になれるでしょうか。
どうしたら、やるべきだけれど困難なことに対して「イエス」と言い、実際にそれを行なうことができるでしょうか。
どうしたら自分にとって最も重要な価値観や大切な人間関係を心にとめ、重要な目標を見失わずにいられるでしょうか。
どうしたら、たとえ気が散るものや誘惑に出合っても、最も大事なことを選択できるようになるのでしょうか。

そうしたことを理解するため、これから「意志力の科学」（著者がスタンフォー

第2章
「めげない人」の体で起きていること

「最高の自分」を引き出すために知っておくべきこと

1. 意志力を発揮できる生理学的状態
2. 筋肉に似ている意志力
3. 将来の自分を大切に
4. 他人からの影響
5. 自分への思いやり

ド大学で受け持っている講座）のなかで私がとくに気に入っている5つの考え方についてお話しします。

私の本（『スタンフォードの自分を変える教室』）を読んでくださった方にとっては、ご存じのこともあるでしょう。

本に出てくる研究事例についても多少お話しします。

友だちにでも再会したような楽しい気持ちで、そうした研究について考え、耳を傾けていただければと思います。

どれも私自身が研究を始めたころ

にあっと驚いた事例です。人は最高の自分を引き出すことができるはずだ、と直観的に思っていただけでなく、科学によってそれが証明されたからです。

科学について多くを学び、脳の働きや環境からの影響についての理解を深め、また私たちの考え方がどのように変わるかを理解するほど、私の考えは変わっていきました。

そうしたことをみなさんにお伝えできるのをうれしく思います。大変なことに取り組んで変化を起こし、最高の自分になることが、少しでも容易になると思うからです。

意志力を発揮できる状態、できない状態

まず、意志力を発揮できるときの生理学的な状態を見てみましょう。

第2章
「めげない人」の体で起きていること

これは私にとって最も重要な科学的洞察でした。

これによって、自分自身や自分の選択のしかたに関する私の考えは、完全に変わりました。

この考え方に従えば、意志力というのは、もっている人ともっていない人がいるというような性質でもなければ、美徳でもなく、脳と体で起こる現象であることがわかります。

そして、意志力を発揮できるときの生理学的な状態、あるいは身体的な反応が、実際にあることがわかります。

意志力は脳と体のなかで起こるものだと理解することは、人間の脳と体が困難に直面したときに示す、ふたつの反応のしかたを理解するのに役立ちます。

では、みなさん、想像してください。

いま、私たちはこのホールにいます。

とても静かで、落ち着いた雰囲気です。

でも、突然、そこのドアからトラが飛び込んできて、ステージをめがけて走ってきたらどうでしょうか。

恐ろしいですね。

そんな異常事態が起きたら、みなさんもパニックになってしまうでしょう。トラは腹ペコで、エサを求めて通路に飛び降りていくかもしれません。

すると、みなさんの体と脳は「闘争・逃走反応」あるいは「ストレス反応」と呼ばれる状態になります。

命が危険にさらされたときに表れる本能です。脳と体は自動的にこのモードに切り替わります。

心臓の鼓動が激しくなり、呼吸も荒く速くなります。冷や汗も出るかもしれません。

目はトラに釘づけになり、必死になってトラの動きを追います。そうやって脳と体のすべてを総動員して、生きるか死ぬかのピンチに立ち向かおうとします。何かあれば瞬時に行動を起こすのです。

第 2 章
「めげない人」の体で起きていること

脳の活動を止めてしまうホルモン

 この闘争・逃走反応は、面白いことに、人がサバイバル本能に従って行動できるよう、「やる力」「やらない力」「望む力」をつかさどる前頭前皮質の活動を停止させてしまいます。

 いっぽう体内では、アドレナリンやコルチゾンなど、闘争・逃走反応に役立つストレスホルモンが放出されます。

 これらのホルモンが循環して脳に戻ってくると、意志力を発揮したり、人生を大きな視野でとらえたりするのに役立つ脳細胞の働きを停止させてしまうのです。生きるか死ぬかの瀬戸際であることを考えれば、納得がいくでしょう。どうしようかなあ、なんて考えていないですぐにでも行動する必要があります。

31

しかし、これから見ていくとおり、何もトラが部屋のなかを走り回っていなくても、脅威や不安などの心理的なストレスを感じると、私たちが最高の自分になろうとする力は妨げられてしまうことがわかります。

私たちを脅かすのは、トラだけではありません。

今晩、家に帰る道すがら、私たちの健康を脅かすような危険が待ち受けているかもしれません——こんなもの（甘いお菓子）が。

とにかく甘いものに目がない人や食べ過ぎで困っている人にとっては、トラが飛び込んでくるより、そのほうがよっぽど恐ろしいかもしれません。

ほかにも誘惑を感じてしまいそうなものがあれば、思い浮かべてみましょう。

おいしそうなお菓子を見かけたとたんに闘争・逃走反応が起こると、自制心など吹っ飛んでしまい、前頭前皮質は活動を停止してしまいます。

そうなったら衝動の命じるまま、お菓子を平らげてしまうかもしれません。

第 2 章
「めげない人」の体で起きていること

この反応を起こせば「理性的」になれる

そういうわけで、長期的な目標を脅かすものに対しては、ちがった反応を起こす必要があります。

生きるか死ぬかのピンチを切り抜けるのとはちがって、このような問題に対処するには、長期的に健康につながるような小さな選択を、日々積み重ねていかなければなりません。

ありがたいことに、私たちには闘争・逃走反応とはまったく逆の本能も備わっているのです。

科学者はこれを「休止・計画反応」と呼んでいます。

長期的な目標に対する脅威を脳が認識した場合――つまり、生死にかかわる危険ではなく、自分にとって最も大事な価値観や目標から離れてしまいそうな危機

を認識すると、脳の状態はさっと切り替わります。心拍数が下がり、呼吸は遅くなります。そして、前頭前皮質にエネルギーが集められます。

ストレス反応とはまさに正反対です。
こうなると、脳はまともな判断ができる状態になります。
「こんなの全部食べちゃったらどうなると思ってるの？　我慢したほうがいいに決まってるじゃない」
つまり、自分に「ノー」と言う「やらない力」が発揮されます。
あるいはまた別の状況で、不安やストレスに襲われたとしても、やるべきことをなしとげるための「やる力」が発揮されます。

第2章
「めげない人」の体で起きていること

「挑戦する人」の生理学的な共通点

休止・計画反応は、意志力がわかりやすいかたちで体に表れたものですが、この反応が起こるのは誘惑を退ける場合に限ったことではありません。

休止・計画反応を解明した研究者たちは、こんな実験を行ないました。

実験のために研究所に集まった参加者の目の前に、クッキーやブラウニーやチョコレートなど、おいしそうなお菓子を山盛りにしたお皿を置きました。

そして、次のように指示しました。

「お菓子は次の実験の参加者用ですので、手をつけないでください。そのかわり、そこに用意したニンジンとセロリのスティックは食べていただいて結構です」

そう言って、担当者は部屋を出て行きました。

この実験では、参加者の心拍数や呼吸などの数値が測定されました。

そして、お菓子の誘惑に打ち勝った参加者の数値を見ると、まさに「休止・計画」の状態に切り替わっていたことがわかりました。
また、別の実験では、課題に失敗した参加者が、否定的なコメントにもめげずに再び課題に取り組んだときにも、その人の体ではまさに同じ反応が起こっていたことがわかりました。

たとえば、ある実験では参加者の女性たちに知能テストを受験させ、その結果について否定的なフィードバックを行ないました。
つまり、大変ひどい成績だったと告げたのです。
そして、こう言いました。
「でも、何度か受験すれば慣れますし、成績がよくなる場合もあります。もういちどやってみますか？」
それに対して、「そうですね、今回はあまりよくできませんでしたが。でも、次はもっとよくできるかもしれないし、やってみます」と、前向きな態度を取る

第2章
「めげない人」の体で起きていること

のはどの参加者か、じつは予想を立てることができました。

つまり、参加者の体に、心拍数が下がったり、呼吸が遅くなったりするような「休止・計画反応」が表れていたかどうかで、どの参加者がもういちど挑戦するかを予想することができたのです。

「依存症」になりやすい人とは？

その他の意志力のチャレンジについても、同じことが確認されています。

たとえば、ある実験では参加者にこう質問しました。

「今日、お金を少しもらうのと、一週間待ってもっとたくさんもらうのと、どちらがいいですか？」

どの参加者が一週間待ってお金をたくさんもらうほうを選ぶか。

それを予想するにも、やはり、心拍数が下がったり、呼吸が遅くなったりした

37

つまり、その人の脳と体には意志力のサインが表れていたわけです。
かどうかがカギでした。

私にとってとくに印象に残ったのは、次のような研究でした。

この実験では、そのようなアルコール依存症の参加者の目の前にお酒を置きました。
参加者は全員アルコール依存症で、断酒を続けようと必死に努力しています。

そして、お酒を見た瞬間に、参加者の体に闘争・逃走反応が表れるか、あるいは休止・計画反応が表れるかを観察しました。

その後、どの参加者が飲酒を再開する可能性があるかについて、予想を立てました。

さらに経過を観察し、どの参加者が実際に断酒に失敗し、またお酒を飲み始めてしまったかを突きとめました。

第2章
「めげない人」の体で起きていること

その結果、お酒という誘惑を目の前にしたときに、体に「闘争・逃走反応」（ストレス反応）が起こるか、あるいは「休止・計画反応」（意志力の反応）が起こるかによって、誰が断酒を破ってしまう可能性が高いか、予想できることがわかったのです。

この研究結果を見て、なるほど、これは使えると私は思いました。呼吸を遅くするといった簡単なことで、自分の体に起こる反応を変えることができるからです。

この「意志力の科学」の実例から私が学んだのは、自分の体に注意を払うことの重要性でした。

体の状態を少し変えるだけで、考え方に大きな変化が表れます。

肝心なときに誘惑に負けたくないと思ったら、わざと呼吸のペースを遅くするなどして、ストレス反応から脱出し、意志力を発揮することができるのです。

あなたはなぜ「リスク」を見きわめられないのか？

体の状態と意志力の関係でもうひとつわかったのは、睡眠を充分にとっていないと、「望む力」をつかさどる脳の部分が働かず、自分にとって最も大事な目標を思い出すことができなくなるということです。

寝不足になると、誘惑がいつもより強烈に感じられ、衝動を抑えにくくなります。

自分の行動があとでどんな影響をもたらすかについて、考えが及ばなくなります。

たとえば、リスクの高い投資案件があっても、リスクを正しく見きわめることができず、儲けが出るのか、損をするのか、まともな判断ができなくなります。

ですから、冴えてる自分になりたいと思ったら、脳を休めるといった単純な方法が効果的な場合もあります。

第 3 章
意志力を「筋肉」のように鍛える秘訣

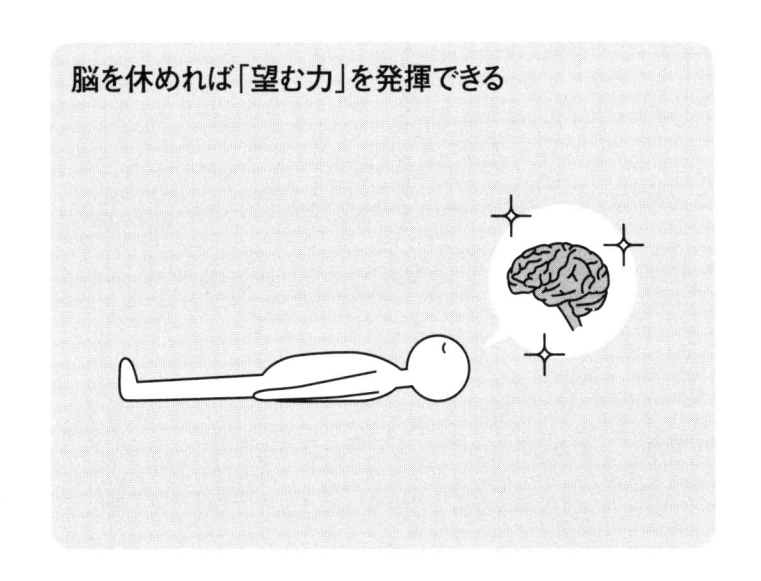

脳を休めれば「望む力」を発揮できる

　また、体のケアやストレス緩和のために行なうさまざまなことが、じつは意志力の保有量を増やす効果があることがわかりました。

　心身を回復させるものは、基本的に意志力の強化に役立ちます。

　けれども、そういうことに時間を使うのは、自分のことだけにかまけているような感じがするかもしれません。

　多くの人は非常に忙しい毎日を送っています。

家族のことや仕事のことで、やるべきことが山ほどあります。なのに、エクササイズや瞑想やヨガをする時間なんてあるわけがない、と思うかもしれません。

しかし、じつはそうやって体を動かすことによって、脳や体が最高の自分を引き出せる状態に切り替わることがわかったのです。

おやつで人の「行動パターン」が変わる

この研究について生物学的な面でもうひとつ驚いたのは、なんと血糖値のレベルも意思決定に影響を与えるという事実です。

食事を抜いたせいで血糖値が下がってしまったり、あるいはジャンクフードなど血糖値が激しく上下するようなものばかり食べたりしていると、最悪の自分になってしまうことがわかりました。

第3章
意志力を「筋肉」のように鍛える秘訣

態度が攻撃的になり、考え方が頑固になり、偏見や先入観にとらわれがちになります。

また、誘惑に負けやすくなり、物事を先延ばしにしがちになります。

ところが興味深いことに、研究者が実験の参加者に血糖値を上げるおやつや飲み物を与えると、参加者の意思決定に変化が表れました。血糖値が上昇した参加者は、将来のために貯金をする割合が増え、ボランティアに使う時間も増えました。

このように、どのくらい前に食事やおやつをとったか、といったささいなことが、人びとの倫理観や選択に影響を与えることを知って、私は驚いてしまいました。

人の血糖値を「操作」してみたら?

では、本には出てこない研究をひとつご紹介しましょう。

イェール大学による最近の研究で、たいへん衝撃的な内容です。

この実験では、研究室に参加者を集め、腕に点滴をしてインスリンとグルコースの注入を行ないました。

それによって、血液中のインスリンとグルコースの濃度を変化させたわけです。

インスリンには血糖を減少させる働きがありますが、グルコースには血液中に糖分を運ぶという逆の働きがあります。

そのようにしてインスリンとグルコースの濃度を変化させながら、参加者の血糖値を刻々と操作しました。

参加者はそうとは知らず、ただじっとしています。

第3章
意志力を「筋肉」のように鍛える秘訣

腕に何を点滴されているのかも知らぬまま、血糖値が上がったり下がったりしています。

そうやって参加者の血糖値を操作しながら、研究者は参加者に色々なものを見せて誘惑し、選択を迫りました。

その結果、血糖値を操作することによって、参加者の意思決定をことごとく操れることがわかったのです。

いま画面に映っているのは、脳の断面図です（DVD参照）。

赤、黄色、オレンジで示された部分は、前頭前皮質です。

ここは意志力の拠点と考えてよいでしょう。

脳のこの部分は血糖値が上がると活発になり、血糖値が下がると活動が鈍くなりました。

いっぽう、血糖値が下がったときに活発になったのは脳の中央の部分です。ここは「衝動的な自己」と結びつき、欲求、誘惑、ストレスに関係しています。

47

こんなふうに血糖値を操作するだけで、人の性格や意思決定に大きな変化が表れるというのは、非常に興味深いことです。

私たちも、自分の血糖値があまり低くならないように注意することによって、自分の感情をコントロールしたり、望ましい選択をしたりすることができるわけです。

以上の例でもわかるとおり、日常生活の小さな選択によって、体内の反応にちがいが表れ、それが自分の考え方や感じ方に大きな影響を及ぼします。

これがみなさんにお伝えしたかった最初のポイントです。

生物学的な観点から自分を見つめ、自分の体をケアする——最高の自分になるために、私たちができる最も重要なことのひとつです。

「小さなステップ」で脳を鍛える

次にご紹介するのは、もっと単純な考え方です。

すなわち、意志力は鍛えることが可能であり、脳はどんなことでも経験を積み重ねることによってうまくなるということです。

筋肉もそうですね。

たとえば上腕二頭筋を鍛えようと思ったら、トレーニングで強化することができます。

重いものを持って、何度か持ち上げます。すると負荷をかけられた筋肉は、もっと簡単に重い物を持ち上げられるようになろうとして強くなります。

体にそのような機能があるのは、私たちもよく知っています。

そして、じつは、脳にも同じような機能があることがわかりました。

学習という行為に最もよく反応する脳の部分は、意志力と自己コントロールを

意志力を鍛えながら前に進む

目標

　意志力について私の考え方が変わるきっかけとなった、ふたつめの考え方をご紹介します。

　以前、私はこう考えていました。

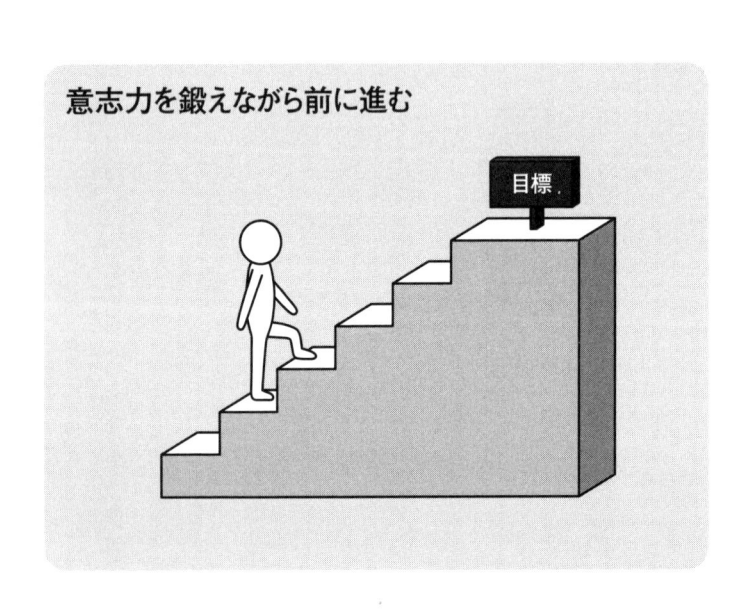

　何か難しいことをやろうとしたり、悪いクセを直そうとしたり、あるいは大変な仕事を始めたりするときには、どのような段取りと方法で取り組むべきかあらかじめ知っておく必要がある。しかも、やるなら一気にやらなければならないと思っていました。

つかさどる部分です。

第3章
意志力を「筋肉」のように鍛える秘訣

けれども、この研究によって私が学んだのは、大きな変化を起こしたり、大きな目標を達成したりするには、目標までの道のりをできるだけ小さなステップに分け、意志力のトレーニングでもするつもりで、小さなステップにしっかり取り組むのが最もよいということでした。

自分がいまできることよりほんの少し難しいことに挑戦していけば、道のりがたやすくなります。

自分には向いていないとか、ほかの人にはできても自分にはできないと思うようなことでも、「禁煙なんて絶対ムリ」とか「あんなこと怖くて絶対にできない」などと思ったとしても、そういうことをなしとげる力は、体を鍛えるのと同じように鍛えることができるのです。

どうしても達成したい目標があるのに、いまの自分にはとても手が届きそうにないと思うなら、体を鍛えるのと同じように、脳と意志力を鍛えようと考えればよいのです。

「20年後」に起きていることを想像してください

次にご紹介する研究については、みなさんにもご自分に照らし合わせて考えていただければと思います。

まず、この図についてご説明しましょう。

これはスタンフォード大学の同僚の研究者が行なった調査研究で、現在の自分と将来の自分とのつながりについて考えるのに役立ちます。

それでは、10年後、あるいは20年後の自分を想像してみましょう。

現在よりも10年ないし20年歳を取った自分の姿はどんな感じか、思い浮かべます。

ここに、ふたつの円の組み合わせが並んでいます。

このなかで、いまのあなたが将来の自分をどれくらい身近に感じ、つながっていると感じるか、あるいはどれくらい似ていると思うか、それを最もよく表して

第3章
意志力を「筋肉」のように鍛える秘訣

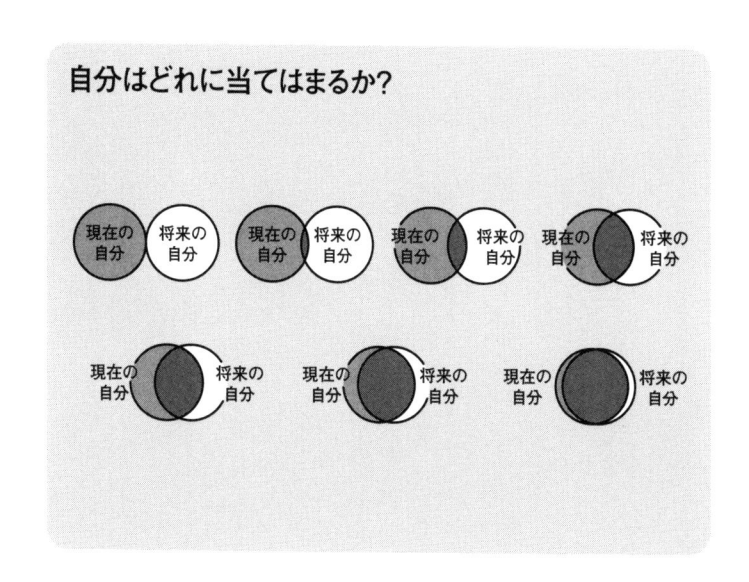

自分はどれに当てはまるか?

（現在の自分／将来の自分の重なり具合を示す7つの図）

いると思う組み合わせをひとつ選んでください。

将来の自分なんて、まるで赤の他人としか思えないでしょうか? その場合は、こちら（左上）のパターンです。

現在の自分は将来の自分のことを別人のようにとらえています。見知らぬ他人も同然です。年老いた姿を想像しても、とても自分とは思えません。

いっぽう、将来の自分とつながっているように感じる人は、こう思う

でしょう。

「そうだな、どんな人か何となくわかるし、どんなことを望んでいるかもわかるような気がする。どんな経験をして、どんなふうに思っているのか、わかるような気がするな」

そして、この右下のパターン（53ページ）は、将来の自分をいまの自分と同じように感じることを表しています。

私自身は、将来の自分をとても身近に感じます。つながっていると感じますし、似ているようにも思います。

みなさんもぜひ考えてみてください。

これらのパターンのうち、どれを選びますか？

10年後、あるいは20年後の自分をどれくらい身近に感じ、つながっている、似ていると感じるでしょうか。

54

第3章
意志力を「筋肉」のように鍛える秘訣

よい「意思決定」ができるパターン

研究者たちは、これらのパターンのうち参加者がどれを選ぶかが、その人の意思決定に深く関わっていることを突きとめました。

理想的には真ん中のパターン、つまり、将来の自分を身近に感じ、つながっているという状態がよいでしょう。

将来の自分のことを責任をもって大事にするべき相手のように感じ、将来の自分が幸せで健康でいられるように気をつけます。

そのいっぽう、将来の自分がいまの自分と完全に同じになるとは思っていないので、将来に向けてよい変化を起こすことも可能だと考えます。

これは、心理学的にとても望ましい状態です。

将来の自分のためになることをしようと思ういっぽうで、変化も可能だという

55

楽天的な心構えでいれば、新しいことにも積極的に挑戦できます。

そして、将来の自分のために投資するようにもなります。

最近では、人びとがそのように将来の自分に関心をもち、つながっているという実感を得られるようにするための実験が、色々と行なわれています。将来の自分を赤の他人のように思ったりせず、現在の自分がもっと素敵になった姿だと思えるようにするためです。

「年老いた自分」と会話する

アメリカに比べて日本ではあまりこうした問題はないようですが、これについてひとつの例をご紹介したいと思います。

アメリカで若い人を対象に行なった実験です。参加者は将来の自分のことを赤の他人と思っているような若い人たちです。

第 3 章
意志力を「筋肉」のように鍛える秘訣

この実験の目的は、若い人が歳を取って退職したころの自分に出会うことができたら、将来のためにもっと貯金をする気になるかどうかを調べることでした。

いま画面に映っているのは、3Dテクノロジーで年老いた自分の姿を見られる装置です（DVD参照）。

この装置をつけると、まるで年老いた自分の三次元のアバターが一緒に部屋にいるように見えます。

私がこの実験に参加したとしましょう。

実験室に入り、椅子に座って、3Dのゴーグルを装着します。

すると、70歳になった私の姿が見えるのです。

私は年老いた自分と見つめ合います。

私が何か言うと、この装置が私の顔の表情や動きをビデオカメラで読み込んで、年老いた私が同じことを言っているように見えます。

実験では、若い人から年老いた自分に対して質問をしたり、話しかけたりしま

した。

たとえば、こんな感じです。

私はこうして座り、年老いた私に向かって尋ねます。

「あなたのお名前は？」

こんどは、年老いた自分になったつもりで答えます。

「ケリーです」

すると、目の前にいる年老いた自分がそう答えたように見えるのです。

実験では、ほかにも色々な質問をしました。

そうやって、年老いた自分と会話をするという貴重な経験ができたわけです。

その後、参加者は一定の予算を与えられ、生活費や貯金などの項目にお金を割り振るという実験に参加しました。

すると、年老いた自分の姿に出会った参加者は、将来の自分の姿を見なかった

第3章
意志力を「筋肉」のように鍛える秘訣

スパッとタバコをやめられる方法

参加者に比べ、２倍の金額を退職後のための貯金へ割り振ったのです。

この実験の話を授業で紹介しはじめたころは、これはテクノロジーとしては面白いけれど、どうやって利用するのだろうと思っていました。

そうしたら、今日、「メリルリンチの広告でこんなのがあります」と学生がメールで教えてくれました。

例の３Dテクノロジーを使ったウェブサイトで、将来の自分の姿に出会える仕組みになっています。

投資家が自分の写真をアップロードすると将来の自分の姿を見ることができます。

そこで、将来に備えて充分な蓄えができるよう、この投資銀行がお手伝いをし

てくれるというわけです。

しかし、これは貯金に限った話ではありません。
将来の自分が健康に長生きできるように気をつけるのにも役立ちます。
ではここで、将来の自分とつながっている実感をもつことの重要性を示す実験を、もうひとつご紹介しましょう。

参加者は喫煙者の女性です。
禁煙したいと思っているのに、どうしてもタバコをやめられません。
研究者はこの女性に、将来の姿をふた通り見てもらいました。
「タバコをやめた場合、10年後のあなたはこうなります」
そして、もうひとつ。
「タバコを吸い続けた場合、10年後のあなたはこうなります」
そして、質問しました。

第3章
意志力を「筋肉」のように鍛える秘訣

「将来のあなたはどんなふうに感じているでしょうか？　体力的にはどうでしょう？　健康状態はどうなっていると思いますか？」

タバコをやめた10年後の女性は、将来の健康と幸せのためにきっぱりとタバコをやめた自分に、感謝しているにちがいありません。

将来を「見る体験」が自分を変える

スタンフォード大学で行なわれた実験をもうひとつご紹介します。

この実験によって、10年後とか50年後とかそんな先の話ではなくても、たとえば来週の自分の姿を見ることができ、短期間でも自分の姿に変化を起こせると思えば、大変なことでもやる気になることがわかりました。

この実験では、参加者はランニングマシーンの上で走ります。

走っていてもいなくても、マシーンに乗った参加者の目には自分のアバターの姿が見えています。

参加者が走るペースを落とすと、アバターの姿は太ってしまいます。

けれども、ペースを上げると、アバターの姿が引き締まってがっしりしてきます。

この実験によって、将来の自分の姿に明らかなちがいが表れるのを見て、実際その通りにちがいないと思った人ほど、長い時間、熱心に走ることがわかりました。

将来の自分について考えるという点において、これらの実験から見えてきたことをまとめると、将来の自分を大切に思い、いま自分が行なうことが将来の自分に跳ね返ってくるのだと考えることが重要です。

自分が選択することの積み重ねは将来の自分をつくるのであり、よくも悪くも自分を大きく変える可能性があるのです。

62

第3章
意志力を「筋肉」のように鍛える秘訣

ですから何をするにしても、自分は将来どうなりたいのか、いまのような選択を続けていったら、10年後、20年後の自分はどう感じるだろうかということを、しっかりと考えてみましょう。

そうすれば、将来のためになることをしようというモチベーションが高まりますし、人はみな変われるのだと思えば励みにもなります。

第 4 章

あなたは「ミラーニューロン」に動かされている

「他人の行動」を変える方法

次はハーバード大学の研究者が発表した画期的な論文です。私も意外に感じたのですが、意志力というのは自己コントロールだけの問題ではないという考えです。

自己コントロールといえば、自分で自分の考えや、行動や、選択をコントロールすることだと思いがちです。

でも、実際には、私たちは他人からの影響を非常に受けていることがわかります。

ハーバード大学の研究によれば、たとえば友人のひとりが太ると、自分も太ってしまう可能性が著しく増加します。

夫や妻、その他の家族でも同様です。

第4章
あなたは「ミラーニューロン」に動かされている

そのようにして肥満率は上昇し、社会的ネットワークのなかで互いに好意をもち、尊敬し合っている仲間のあいだで、さらに肥満が広まっていきます。

このように意志力にまつわる失敗例として、研究者が最初に観察したのが肥満でした。

けれども、意志力の成功も同じように広まることがわかったのです。たとえば仲間の誰かがタバコをやめると、その人の友人や家族もタバコをやめる確率が高くなります。

このように、研究者たちは意志力に関するさまざまな行為に同様のパターンが見られることを発見しました。

飲酒や浪費などもそうです。

あるいは、助け合いが広まった例もあります。

誰かがもっと他人の立場になり、思いやりをもって行動しようと決心します。

すると、そのような振る舞いが社会的ネットワークを通して広まっていくのです。これは非常に有益で、心にとめておくべき重要な考えだと思います。私たちの選択はそれだけ周りの人に影響を及ぼし、また、私たち自身も周りの人の影響を受けているということです。

「自己」の認識には「好きな人」も入っている

成功にしても失敗にしても、意志力はなぜ感染するのだろう、と私は考えるようになりました。

そして、やはり、脳の働きに興味をもちました。

そこで、私たちがなぜ他人の影響を受けやすいのかを理解するために、神経科学の考え方をふたつご紹介したいと思います。

ひとつは、私たちが自分について考えるときには、じつは自分のことだけを考

第4章
あなたは「ミラーニューロン」に動かされている

えているのではない、ということです。

興味深いことに、私たちが認識する自己という感覚には、ほかの人たち、とりわけ、自分が大切に思っている人たちも含まれています。

いまご覧になっているスライド（DVD参照）には脳の画像が映っていますが、左右で異なる種類の断面図になっています。

わかりやすくご説明しましょう。

このように立っている私の頭を巨大な刃物で縦に真っ二つに切ったものと想像してください。そうすると、脳のなかがこんなふうに見えます（左側の断面図）。

このあたりは「望む力」をつかさどる脳の部分です。

自分にとって最も大事な目標や価値観を覚えているのは、この部分です。

そして、自分はどういう人間かという自己認識を行なうのも、脳のこの領域です。これ（左上の画像の赤い部分）は、自分自身のことを考えたときに、脳のこの部分が活発になったことを示しています。

いっぽう、左下は、母親のことを考えたときに活発になった部分を示しています。

このふたつはとても似ていますね。

他人のことを考えたときには、脳のほかの部分が活発になります。

興味深いことに、私たちは自分にとって大切な人のことを考えているときには、自分のことも考えています。

私たちは他人との関係や、他人とのつながりにおいて自分が果たす役割をとおして、自分が何者であるかを認識しています。

それはすなわち、自分の「望む力」にはほかの人も関わってくるということです。

たとえば、ほかの人が好きだと言った何かが、いつのまにか自分の目標や価値観のなかに組み込まれていたりします。

そのようにして、私たちはほかの人の意志力の成功や失敗に感染します。

自分の好きな人が何か変化を起こすと、脳が自動的にその人の変化なり目標を

第4章
あなたは「ミラーニューロン」に動かされている

自分のものとして取り込んでしまうわけです。

無意識に影響を受けてしまう

また、人間の脳にはミラーニューロンと呼ばれる細胞が数多く存在することもわかっています。

この細胞は他人が考えていることや感じていることに対してつねに注意を払っています。

ミラーニューロンの働きによって、私たちはほかの人の意志力に感染したり、また自分の意志力がほかの人にうつったりするのです。

たとえば、一緒にいた誰かが何かの誘惑に負けてしまったのを見たとします。

すると、私たちの脳はその人が何かしたことを自動的に理解しようとします。

つまり、まるで自分も同じことをしたかのような感覚を脳がつくりだすのです。

みなさんにもきっと似たような経験があるのではないでしょうか。

大切な人が痛い思いをしたり、パニック状態になったりすると、自分も同じような感覚に襲われます。自分も痛みを感じたかのように体がビクッとしたり、気が動転してしまったり。

どうやら、それと同じことが目標や意志力についても起こるようなのです。身近に意志の強い人がいると、自分もそれに感染します。

同様に、ストレスのせいで自制心の利かない人が周りにいると、自分もそんな気分になってしまいます。

そこで私は、自分自身をどれだけコントロールできているか、と自制心にだけ注目するのではなく、自分が社会的な環境からどれだけ影響を受けているかについても注目すべきだと考えるようになりました。

また、社会的な環境に対して自分はどのような貢献をしているかも意識する必

第4章
あなたは「ミラーニューロン」に動かされている

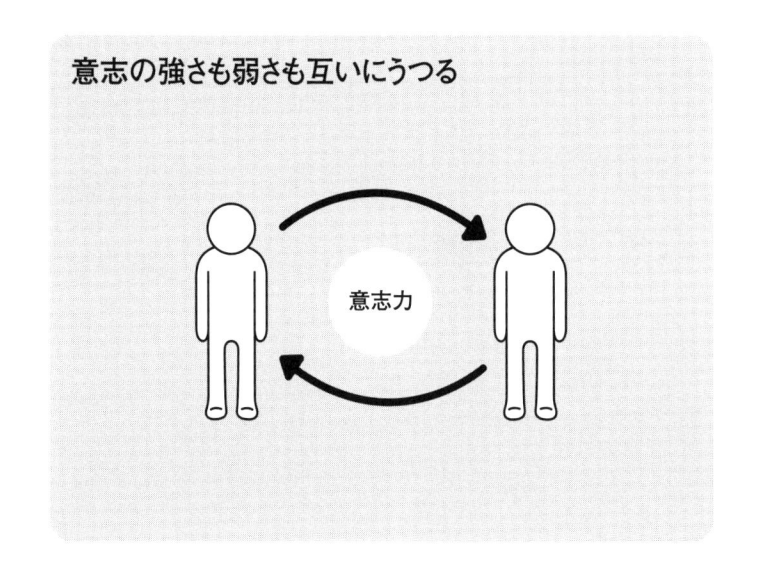

意志の強さも弱さも互いにうつる

意志力

要があります。

そのように両面から考えることによって、自分自身や周りの人をサポートするためにどんなことができるかについて、考え方を広げることができました。

「思い浮かべる」だけで意志力が強くなる

私がいつもお勧めしているのは、まず、よいことにしろ、悪いことにしろ、自分がお手本にしている人は

誰だろう、と考えてみることです。

自分が影響を受けている人、また逆に自分の影響を受けやすい人は誰だろう。自分が真剣に取り組みたいと思っている目標や価値観を共有している人は誰だろう。自分の目標を応援してくれる人は誰だろう、と考えてみましょう。

そのような人間関係を認識して深めていくのはとても大事で、自己コントロールの強化にも役立ちます。

挫けそうになったときや疲れたときでも、そのように同じ目標に取り組んでいる仲間や応援してくれる人のことを考えるだけで意志力が強くなることが、研究によって明らかになっています。

また、自分が行なうことは大切な人たちにもよい影響をもたらすだろうと考えるのもよいことです。

自分のためだと思うとやる気が起きないことでも、ほかの人のためと思えばが

第4章
あなたは「ミラーニューロン」に動かされている

んばれたりするからです。

このように、自分のためにすることは大切な人のためにもなると認識することも、自制心を発揮するために大いに役立ちます。

「拷問テスト」とは何か？

それでは、拷問テストの話をしましょう。

授業でこの実験について話し合うと、だいたい議論になります。

というのも、一般的に自己コントロールを強化するために必要だと思われていることとは、逆の考え方だからです。

それは、自分を批判したり恥に思ったり、罪悪感を抱いたりするよりも、自分に対して思いやりをもったほうが、はるかに自己コントロールを発揮することができるという考え方です。

実際、罪悪感や恥の意識や自己批判のせいで自己コントロールが弱くなることはあっても、強くなることはありません。

自分を許し、自分の抱えているストレスや苦しみ、そして自分の弱ささえも受け入れることで、私たちは強くなれるのです。

そのことを示す例をふたつご紹介しましょう。

最初にご紹介する実験には、拷問テストが登場します。

この実験では、禁煙を考えている参加者に対し、実験前の12時間はタバコを吸わないように指示しました。

ですから、参加者はみんなタバコを吸いたくてたまらない状態になっていました。

研究室に集まった参加者は、各自好きな銘柄のタバコを持参しました。

もちろん、ライターもです。

第4章
あなたは「ミラーニューロン」に動かされている

なにしろ喫煙に関する実験ですから、すぐにでもタバコが吸えるだろうと思っていました。

2時間「ストップ」を繰り返す

ところが、研究者は参加者をある部屋に閉じ込め、ゆっくりと拷問テストを行なったのです。

まず、「タバコの箱を取り出して、手に持ってください」と指示がありました。

参加者はひそかに喜びます。

「やった、ようやく一服できる」

しかし、インターホンから指示が響きます。

「ストップ」

この声がしたら、参加者はどのくらいタバコを吸いたいと思っているか、そし

て、タバコを吸えないことでどの程度のストレスを感じているかを、評価表に記入しなければなりません。

次の指示まで2分待ちました。
すると、また指示が聞こえます。
「では、タバコの箱のセロファンをはがしてください」
参加者は喜びます。
「よかった。やっと吸えるのか」
みんなセロファンをはがします。すると、インターホンの声が響きました。
「ストップ」
また、評価表に記入します。
やがて、また指示が聞こえました。
「タバコを1本、箱から出してください」
参加者は指示に従います。

第4章
あなたは「ミラーニューロン」に動かされている

なぜ、喫煙量が40％も激減したのか？

「ストップ」
「では、タバコの匂いをかいでください」
「ストップ」
「それでは、タバコを口にくわえてください」
「ストップ」
「ライターを持ってください」
「ストップ」

この調子で延々と2時間も続きました。拷問テストと呼ばれるゆえんです。

これが意志力の強化に役立つ実験だと言えるのは、この実験のおかげで参加者のうち何人かは、タバコを吸いたい欲求とタバコを吸えないストレスに対処する

ための戦略を学んだからです。

タバコを吸いたくなるとどういう感じがするか、タバコを吸いたいのに吸えないのはどんなにつらいかを、まざまざと体で実感する。そして、吸いたいのに吸えないつらさを、自分への思いやりをもってじっと見つめるという方法です。

このように、自分に対する思いやりをもちながら、自分の感じている欲求や苦しみにじっと注意を払うという方法を学んだ人たちは、タバコの量を減らすように指示されたわけでもないのに、実験を行なった次の週の喫煙量が40％も減ったことがわかりました。

自分の感じている欲求やストレスを受けとめる方法を学んだことによって、以前よりも禁煙という目標に従って行動できるようになったわけです。

このように、大変なことに取り組むときには自分に思いやりをもつようにするのも、意志力を強化する方法のひとつです。

第4章
あなたは「ミラーニューロン」に動かされている

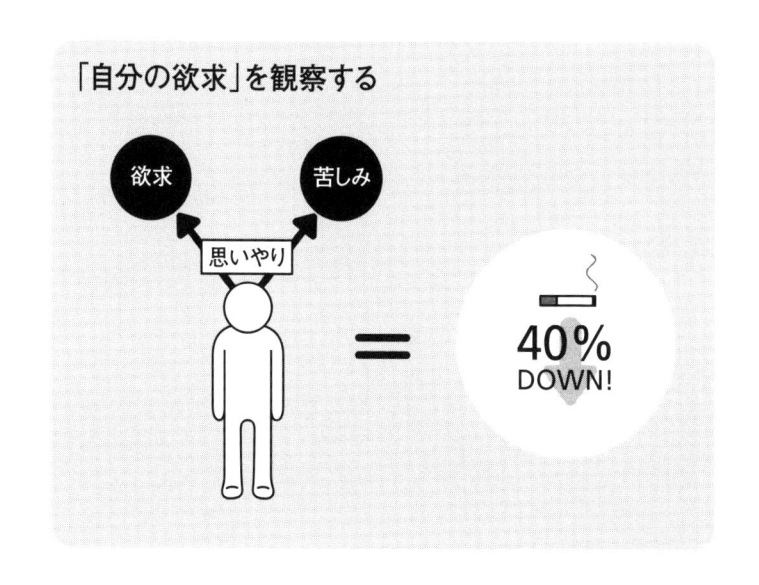

「自分の欲求」を観察する

欲求 　苦しみ
思いやり

＝ 40% DOWN!

脳に「欲求」と「行動」をつなげさせない

同じ方法を用いた研究をもうひとつご紹介します。

やはり参加者はタバコをやめたいと思っているのに禁煙できない人たちです。

この実験では、タバコを吸いたい欲求と吸いたいのに吸えないストレスに対し、自分に対する思いやりをもって対処した場合、脳ではどのような反応が起こるかを調べました。

まず、参加者は脳スキャナーに入ります。例の方法を試したときに脳でどのような変化が起こるかを観察するためです。

脳スキャナーに入った参加者は、喫煙に関するさまざまな画像を見せられます。好きなタバコをやめようとしている人がそんな画像を見せられたら、タバコが吸いたくなるに決まっています。

この実験では、参加者は自分の欲求を素直に受けとめてじっと見つめながらも、自分に対して思いやりをもつ、という方法を試すように指示されました。

ところが、ときにはわざとそのような方法をとらずにふつうにしてください、という指示も出されました。

その結果、参加者が自分の欲求を受けとめて、じっと見つめ、自分に対して思いやりをもつという態度で臨んだときには、タバコを吸いたい欲求が弱まり、ストレスも和（やわ）らいだことがわかりました。

このとき脳ではどのような反応が起こっていたかというと、ストレスや欲求に

第4章
あなたは「ミラーニューロン」に動かされている

関連する領域の活動が鈍くなっていたのがわかりました。

さらに重要なことに、ストレスや欲求に関わる脳の領域と、欲求に反応して行動を起こさせる脳の領域との連絡が、途絶えていたことがわかったのです。

第 5 章

私がいちばん
使っている方法

欲求を静かに見つめる

前運動皮質は、これからしようとすることを計画する脳の領域です。喫煙者がタバコを吸いたい欲求を感じると、脳のこの部分が「ポケットに手を伸ばしてタバコとライターを取れ」という命令を出します。欲求を感じた瞬間には命令を出しているほどです。

しかし、研究で明らかになったとおり、欲求やストレスを感じたときに、自分への思いやりをもちながらじっと注意を払っていると、反射的な行動をするための脳内の連絡が途絶えます。

そのせいで欲求やストレスを感じていても、すぐに反射的な行動を起こさなくなります。

じつに思いがけないことです。

第5章
私がいちばん使っている方法

ふつうはストレスや欲求を感じたら、ああ、困ったと思って、とりあえず忘れようとするでしょう。

何かで気を紛（まぎ）らわせたり、逃避したりします。

そういう態度ではなく、苦しんでいる自分に手を差しのべるような、あるいはつらい思いをしている自分の友だちになったつもりになるのです。

このテクニックは喫煙者だけでなく、ダイエットや過食など食べ物に関する問題を抱えている人にも効果があるとわかっています。

アルコールや薬物の依存症に苦しんでいる人、不安障害で悩んでいる人にも効果があることがわかっています。

この方法を使うと恐怖や不安を感じても、思いやりのあるやさしい態度で向き合えるようになります。

心のなかのストレスや苦しみに注意を向けているうちに、ストレスや苦しみが少しずつ和らいでいきます。

そうやって心のゆとりを取り戻すことにより、自分の目標にふさわしい行動を

取れるようになります。

失敗を気にすればするほど意志力は下がる

今日ご紹介したさまざまな方法のなかでも、いまお話ししたのは、私がふだん最もよく利用している方法です。

心のなかの葛藤や苦しみを取り除くことはできなくても、自分自身の友だちになったつもりでそれを受けとめるようにすると、大事な目標にふさわしい行動を取れるようになります。

不安にかられて行動したり、誘惑に負けたり、欲求のままに行動したりしなくなるのです。

では、自分に思いやりをもったときに脳ではどんなことが起こるかというと、

第5章
私がいちばん使っている方法

前頭前皮質が働くようになります。

いまご覧いただいている画像（DVD参照）は、失敗をしたときに罪悪感を抱いたり自分を恥じたりした場合、脳ではどんな反応が起こるかを示したものです。

意志力をつかさどる前頭前皮質が、ストレスや不安や欲求や衝動を生み出す脳の領域を統制することができなくなったことを示しています。

失敗を恥じたり、罪悪感を抱いたりすると、意志力が奪われてしまうのです。

そうすると、同じ失敗を繰り返したり、またしても欲求に負けて落ち込んだりするはめになります。

けれども、自分に思いやりをもてば、それとは逆のことが起こるのです。

「自分と対話する」ための戦略

最後にみなさんにご紹介したいのは、つらい思いをしているときに自分に対し

て思いやりをもつための実践的な戦略です。

誘惑や不安に悩んでいるとき。あるいは何か失敗をしたり、誰かをがっかりさせてしまったりして、罪悪感に苛(さいな)まれ、自分を恥じ、自分を許せないでいるとき。

「もうあの人との関係を修復するのはムリだろう」とか、「もうあの目標を達成するのはムリだろう」と諦(あきら)めかけているような状況です。

そんなとき、「思いやりの科学」(著者がスタンフォード大学で受け持っている講座のひとつ)ではこんな方法を用います。

シンプルな3つのステップにしたがって、自分自身と対話をするのです。

1つめのステップでは、心のなかで感じていることを、すべてありのままに見つめます。

喫煙者がタバコを吸いたいと思ったときに、自分への思いやりをもって、やさしい態度で受けとめようとしたのと同じです。

90

第5章
私がいちばん使っている方法

自分に対する失望や自信のなさ、あるいは後悔といった感情から目をそむけずに、素直に感じてみます。

そうすると、激しい感情やつらさに呑み込まれてしまったりせずに、落ち着いてやさしい気持ちで自分を見つめ、つらい気持ちを受けとめられるようになります。

2つめのステップでは、どんなにつらいとしても、つらい思いをしているのは自分だけではない、ということを思い出します。

たとえどんな失敗をしても、あるいは望ましくない欲求を抱いてしまい罪悪感に苛まれたとしても、それは人間らしいことであって、自分がダメな人間だからではないのです。

人は誰でも失敗をします。挫折(ざせつ)もするし、あやまちも犯します。

けれども、ストレスを感じるときやつらいときには、ついそのことを忘れてしまいます。

あやまちを犯すのはいかに人間らしいことかを忘れてしまうと、もういちど目標に取り組もうとする意志力を失ってしまいます。

しかし、研究で明らかになっているとおり、人は誰でもあやまちを犯すことを忘れずにいられれば、自分のあやまちも人間らしさの表れであり、何も自分だけがそういう欠点を抱えているわけではないとわかります。

そうすると、もういちど目標に向き合って、取り組めるようになります。

3つめのステップでは、大切な人に話しかけるつもりで、自分に話しかけます。目標を諦めかけている友人や、挫けそうになっている友だちに言葉をかけるとしたら、どんなことを言うだろうかと考えてみます。

そして、自分をその友人の立場に置き換えてみるのです。

私たちはつい自分のことを批判的な目で見てしまったり、大切な人になら決して言わないような言葉で自分をののしったりしてしまいますが、そういう態度に陥（おちい）らないようにします。

第 5 章
私がいちばん使っている方法

自分に「思いやり」を向けるには?

1 気を紛らわしたりせず、ストレスや苦しみに注意を払う

2 「こんなふうに悩んでいるのは自分ひとりではない」と思い出す

3 「大切な人に対してなら、どんな言葉をかけるか」と考える

よい自分になるための「5つの考え方」

それでは、質疑応答へ移るまえに、まとめをしたいと思います。

今日は「意志力の科学」から、よい自分になるための5つの考え方をご紹介しました。

さまざまな戦略があり、難しい問題にも色々な取り組み方ができることがわかりました。

まず、自分の体に目を向け、睡眠時間を増やしたり、運動をしたり、呼吸を遅らせるといった単純なことで、自分の考え方や選択に変化が表れることがわかりました。

まったく別の方法としては、誰かにサポートを頼んだり、大切な人との結びつきを強化したりすることで、意志力を強化することもできます。同時に、相手がチャレンジに取り組む手伝いをすることもできるでしょう。

そして、自分自身のことをどのように考えているかが、意思決定に大きく影響することも学びました。

よい自分になるためのひとつの方法は、こうなりたいと思う将来の自分の姿を想像することです。

将来の自分の姿をまざまざと思い描くことによって、自己コントロールが強化されます。

ご紹介したさまざまな方法のうちどれから始めても、意志力を強化することができます。

第5章 私がいちばん使っている方法

「自分の知らない自分」を見つける

最後に、ぜひみなさんの心にとめておいていただきたいポイントをご紹介します。

「意志力の科学」の講座で紹介している方法ですが、みなさんがこれから色々な経験をしていくなかで、自分自身を支えるために役立つと思います。

ひとつは、科学者になったつもりで考えることです。

科学者は実際に起きている現象を、偏見（へんけん）をもたずに好奇心をもって観察します。物事がどのような仕組みで働くかにとても興味があり、自分自身でさえその興味の対象になります。

みなさんも科学者になったつもりで自分自身をじっと観察し、どういう仕組みになっているのか解き明かしてみましょう。

理解を深めるにつれ、その仕組みをうまく利用できるようになります。自分自身を対象に意志力の実験を行なっていると考えれば、新しい考え方や行動のしかたを色々試し、その結果を観察することができます。最初から正しい方法がわからなくても、あれこれと実験を行なって探ってみるのも楽しいものです。

自分を対象に実験を行ない、生活を実験の場として活用しましょう。自分にとって最も役に立つ方法を見つけるために、さまざまな戦略を試してみてください。

また、私がいつもお勧めしているのは、自分のさまざまな側面を知ることです。今日の講演で最初にお話ししたのは、心のなかにはつねに葛藤がある、相反するふたつの自己が存在し、時間の使い方や意思決定をめぐってせめぎ合っているという考えでした。

私自身の経験からも言えることですが、あまり感心できないようなことをしよ

第5章
私がいちばん使っている方法

「悩むこと」「苦しむこと」は当たり前

うとする自分も含め、色々な自分を理解するうちに、もっとほかにどんな側面があるのか知りたくなります。

そうやって自覚を深めるほど、どんな自分になるかを選択できるようになるわけです。

最後にお勧めしたいのは、人間はみな同じだということを忘れないことです。自分のことをよく観察し、頭の働きについて理解を深めるほど、ほかの人たちのこともわかってきます。

悩んでいるのはみんな一緒なんだ、と理解することは、意志力と自己コントロールの最大の源にもなります。

誰でもストレスで苦しんだり、物事を先延ばしにしたり、将来のための努力を

怠ったりして悩んでいます。誘惑に苦しんだり、自分では抑えられない感情に悩まされたりもしています。

それも人間らしい当たり前のことだと思えば自分だけがどうしようもないわけではないのだとわかります。

自分のことがよくわかってくると、ほかの人たちとつながっている感じがして、たとえ苦しくても、あまり孤独だと感じなくなります。

苦しみのなかでほかの人たちとのつながりを感じることで、意志力が最大限に引き出されるのです。

大変なチャレンジであっても、みんなとつながっている、ひとりではないんだと実感できれば、新たなチャレンジに取り組む意欲が湧いてくるでしょう。

以上をもって、みなさんにお礼申し上げます。ありがとうございました。

第 6 章

日本のみなさんの疑問に答えます

上手に「ものの見方を変える」にはどうすればいいですか？

Q ケリー先生のお話を聞いて、意志力を使うには視点の切り替えがとても大切だと思ったのですが、視点の切り替えをうまく行なう方法はありますか？

ケリー：そうですね。どうやってものの見方を変えるか、ということですね。意外なことに、考え方を変えようとするよりも、体の状態を変えたほうがうまくいく場合もあります。

体の状態が変化すると、思いがけず、それまでとはちがったものの見方ができるようになったりします。

たとえば、呼吸に意識を集中したり、呼吸を意識しながら瞑想を行なったり。

第6章
日本のみなさんの疑問に答えます

自分の考え方を変えようなんてことは考えず、ただゆっくりと呼吸をしながら心を静めていきます。

そうすると、知恵が浮かぶというか、物事がはっきりと見えてきて、新しいとらえ方ができるようになり、大変なことに取り組むのに役立ちます。

ですから、ものの見方を変えるのに最もよい方法は、自分自身の考えと闘ったりすることではなく、新しい考え方が生まれるような、心と体のゆとりをつくりだすことだと思います。

今日の講演ではお話しできませんでしたが、ある研究によって、頭のなかで考えていることをコントロールするのは非常に困難であることがわかっています。考え方を変えようと思うほど、かえってその考え方にとらわれてしまうのです。

これは「皮肉なリバウンド効果」と呼ばれており、何かについて考えないようにしようとすればするほど、そのことばかり考えてしまいます。

ですから、ものの見方を変えたいと思ったら、むしろ体の状態を変化させて心を落ち着けるという、いわば裏ワザを使うのがいちばんよいと思います。

あるいはものの見方を変えるといっても、新しい服を試着するようなものだと思えば、気楽にできるかもしれません。

自分がお手本にしている人のことを考えて、その人だったらこの問題にどう対処するだろう、と想像してみるのもよい方法です。

たとえば自信のないとき、もっと自信をもち、勇気を出してがんばりたいと思ったら、勇気のある人のことを思い出し、あの人だったらこの問題をどう考えるだろうと想像して、自分も同じように考えてみるのです。

言ってみれば、これも意志力の実験のようなものです。

第6章
日本のみなさんの疑問に答えます

Q 「科学」によって意志力の「何」がわかりましたか？

意志というのは哲学などの学問で扱うことが多いと思うのですが、科学や心理学で意志力を扱いはじめたケリー先生は、それによってどういうことがわかってきたでしょうか？

ケリー：とても興味深いことですね。ひとつ確実に言えることは、知恵と呼ばれるものの多くは哲学や宗教からきていますが、科学は基本的にそれらの考え方を支持しています。

一般的な考え方のなかにも、科学的に反証されたものより、むしろ証明された例がたくさんあります。

ですから、ある意味では、科学は物事を考えるためのひとつの方法であり、哲

103

学や宗教などの知恵になじみのない人に考えを伝える方法でもあると言えるでしょう。

けれども、哲学や宗教などの思想について、科学が解き明かしてくれたこともあるのです。

とくに神経科学によって、私は哲学やその他の伝統的な考え方とはちがう視点を得ることができたと感じています。

そのひとつが、私たちのなかには複数の自己がいて、それらがしょっちゅう切り替わるということです。

哲学でもこうした考え、つまり、私たちのなかには複数の自己が存在し、人間はさまざまな困難に対して柔軟に対応できるということは認識していますが、そのことについて深く掘り下げてはいません。

でも、脳の反応を見れば明らかにわかります。

第6章
日本のみなさんの疑問に答えます

たとえば、先ほどご紹介した研究のように血糖値を操作すると、その人の性格や意思決定に著しい変化が表れました。

そのことを知ったおかげで、私は自分への思いやりや理解を深めることができました。

哲学にはすばらしい考え方がたくさんありますが、このことについては、私は科学から学びました。

ですから科学は物事について考えるためのひとつの方法になると思いますが、だからといって科学は哲学や宗教などに取ってかわるものではないと思います。

脳科学を「ビジネスに生かす」にはどうすればいいですか？

Q お話をうかがい、脳科学は興味深い研究結果を私たちに与えてくれると改めて思いました。いっぽうで、そうした研究を深めていくためには研究資金が必要になってくるという側面もあるかと思います。それを考えたときに、脳科学を企業の成長に生かすなどビジネスにつなげることも重要かと思うのですが、どのようなことが可能か、ご意見をうかがわせてください。

ケリー：素晴らしいご質問ですね。私が住んでいるカリフォルニア州のシリコンバレーでは、すでにそうした取り組みが始まっています。私自身も研究に参加しており、今日お話ししたような研究のテクニックを企業で教えています。

106

第6章
日本のみなさんの疑問に答えます

たとえば、グーグル社で行なっているトレーニングプログラムでは、従業員に瞑想やストレス緩和、思いやりのスキルを教えています。

シリコンバレーの企業の多くは、そうしたことによって従業員の生産性がいかに向上し、会社に対する満足度が高まるかを認識しています。

多くの企業では通常の勤務時間内にそのようなトレーニングを行なう取り組みを始めています。ストレスを緩和するためのツールを従業員に提供する必要があるからです。

瞑想のための部屋を設けて、従業員が脳を鍛え、意志力を回復できるようにしています。

現在、各企業がスポンサーとなって資金を提供し、研究グループがさまざまな方法を試しているところです。

そうした研究の結果が発表されるようになれば研究費も増え、さらに優れた方

法を見つけることができるでしょう。

そうやって、研究者たちがつねに色々な方法を試して比較するということが必要です。最もよい方法を見つけるまでにはまだ道のりは遠いかもしれませんが、少なくともアメリカではすでに取り組みが始まっています。

「将来の自分」をイメージする方法を教えてください

Q「自分の将来の姿をイメージする」というお話が出てきましたが、先生のお話に出てきたようなシミュレーションの機械は身近にはありません。そういう場合、どうすれば少しでも自分の将来をイメージできるか、具体的な方法があったら教えてください。

みなさんの疑問に答えます

ケリー……まず言えるのは、意志力を鍛えるにあたっては、難しいことほど効果があるということです。

将来の自分の姿を見て、語り合うことができるなんて、あれは本当にすごいテクノロジーだと思います。

けれども、そういう方法以外に、将来の自分とつながる方法を見つけようと努力すれば、結果的に実りはもっと大きくなります。

なぜなら、そのようなメンタルな戦略を身につけることができるからです。

意志力に関する基本的な考え方として、難しいことを継続して行なうほど、大きな効果が得られます。

私が授業で学生にやってもらうエクササイズのひとつに、将来の自分から現在の自分に宛てた手紙を書くというのがあります。感謝の手紙です。

いま一生懸命に取り組んでいる目標をついに達成した自分の姿や、現在抱えて

いる難しい問題を克服した姿を想像して、将来の自分から現在の自分へ、がんばってくれてありがとう、おかげで困難を乗り越えることができたよ、と感謝の手紙を書くのです。

たとえ将来の自分が書いているようなつもりにはなりきれなかったとしても、いまちゃんとこれをやっておこう、という具体的なアイデアを得ることができます。

ある意味では、現在の自分が最高の自分になるための方法と言えるでしょう。このエクササイズはとてもお勧めです。

ほかにも科学者がよく行なうエクササイズで、将来の自分の気持ちを想像することによって、想像力を鍛えるという方法もあります。

将来の自分とのつながりを感じるのが難しいのは、将来の自分の気持ちを実感するのが難しいせいもあるでしょう。

そこで、将来の自分を想像するときには、外見を想像するよりも、将来の自分

第6章
日本のみなさんの疑問に答えます

は何を大切に思っているだろう、どんなことを望んでいるだろう、と考えてみるのです。

将来の自分の姿はあまり想像できないとしても、このようなシミュレーションを行なえば、長い目で見た場合、最も大きな効果を発揮します。

　　　　＊

最後に、みなさんにメッセージを贈ります。

とにかく、始めましょう。

何をしたらよいかよくわからなくても、自分の思い描く大きなビジョンや変化につながりそうな小さな一歩を見いだして、とにかくやってみましょう。

そこから必ず道が開けていくと信じて。

in any way consistent with the big vision or the big change, and just begin, and trust the process that will enfold from that.

to do today that allowed you to handle that challenge. That particular type of letter, even if it does not feel like your future self, you end up coming up with ideas for actually what you are willing to do now. In a way, it allows you to tap into the best version of your present self. That is one exercise that I like to have people do.

Another exercise that scientists have used is to have people strengthen the muscle of fantasy by thinking about inner experiences in the future. One of the reasons why it is hard to connect to people's future self often is it is hard to generate what your emotions will be in future. When you think about your future self, rather than trying to think about what that future self will look like, to really think about what that person might care about and what that person might want. That is the kind of simulation that ends up being most powerful in the long term, even if you do not know what your future self is going to look like.

*

To give you one last word, begin, when you do not know what else to do, find the absolute smaller step that you can take that is

A 4

Kelly McGonigal

One thing I will say right off the bat is sometimes the things that are harder are more effective when it comes to training willpower. So, even though it is really fun to see yourself, to actually have a picture of yourself and interact with that person, that technology is really cool. In some ways what it takes to struggle, to find a way to connect to your future self is probably going to be more rewarding down the road because it is going to then become a mental strategy that you will have. That is a basic idea of willpower in general, that the harder it is to do it, probably the more beneficial it is to persist that.

One of the exercises that I have my students do in class is to write a letter from their future self to their present self, and specifically a letter of gratitude, to imagine yourself at some point in the future where you have reached some goal that you are struggling with now or you have overcome some very difficult situation that you are living through right now, and to write a letter to yourself thanking you for what you were willing involved in research studies where we are teaching people some of the techniques that I talked about today in work places, for example, at Google, we have a training program that we do there, teaching people meditation and stress reduction, as well as compassion skills. Many of the companies in Silicon Valley have recognized how much this improves people's productivity and their satisfaction with their employer.

Many companies have begun to include them as part of everyday office activities that you know we need to give people tools for stress reduction; we need to have a meditation room so that people can train their brains and restore their willpower.

Right now I think that the research is at that level where individual companies are helping to sponsor studies where research groups can come in and try out different strategies. I think that as those findings start to become published, there is going to be more research funds available to figure out how to do it well. That is one of things that we need to where the researchers always test out different strategies against each other. We are a long way off from knowing the best way to do that, but I think that it is already happening in the States.

learned in philosophy or in other traditions, one of them is this idea of how quickly we shift back and forth between different versions of ourselves. Sometimes in philosophy there is not an appreciation of the value of the different version of ourselves and how flexible we are as humans in responding to different challenges.

I think sometimes just seeing that in the brain. For example, the study I showed you about how when the blood sugar levels are manipulated, it radically changed people's personality and their choices. That is something that has given me a sense of self compassion and understanding that I have not necessarily received from philosophies that have a lot of great other ideas to share. I think that it becomes just another source of ideas and not something that is going to necessarily replace them.

A 3

Kelly McGonigal

Yes, that is a great question. Where I live in California, in Silicon Valley this is already being done. I myself have been person think about this challenge and try it on for yourself. In that way, it is like a willpower experiment.

A 2

Kelly McGonigal

Yeah, I think this is really interesting. One of the things I will say for sure is that a lot of the things you might think of as wisdom coming out of philosophy or coming out of contemplative traditions and religions. Science is basically supporting a lot of those ideas. There are a lot of ideas that we have heard before that seem to be confirmed by science rather than refuted by science. So, in some ways science becomes another way to think about a problem and another way to communicate that to people who may have not been exposed to philosophy or not interested in the wisdom traditions. But I will say that there are some aspects of science that have clarified ideas that I might have seen in philosophy or in other traditions.

In particular, I feel like the neuroscience has changed the way that I think about some problems from how I might have the wisdom or clear thinking that is going to be helpful for meeting a certain challenge.

Sometimes I think one of the best ways is to change your own perspective, is to rather than struggle with your own thoughts and fight with your own thoughts, to create a state and a space for new perspective to arise. One of the areas of research, I did not get to talk about tonight is research on how difficult it is to control our thoughts. Sometimes the more we try to change the way we are thinking, the more we get stuck in the way that we are thinking. It is called an ironic rebound where the more you try not to think something, the more likely you are to think it.

I think that sometimes the best way to change a perspective is to be sneaky about it, like to change the state of your body and slow down the mind or maybe to think about new perspective as being like a new outfit you could try on, not to be so serious about it, and to think about a role model and how they might think about a challenge. What would it be like? For example, if somebody is feeling self-doubt and needs to try on the perspective of self confidence or courage to think about someone you know who is courageous, and think, well, how would that challenges connect us to others rather than isolate us from others, that is often what we need to find the willingness to take on the next challenge.

With that, I want to say thank you. Arigato.

Chapter 6

A 1

Kelly McGonigal

Yes. This idea that how do I change my perspective? One of the things that surprises me is sometimes you do not have to try to change the way you are thinking, but you can change something like what is happening in your body and then often, it gives rise to a new perspective that was not previously available, something like focusing on the breath, breath focus meditation where you are not intentionally trying to change your perspective, but you are slowing down your breath and you are quieting the mind, often a new perspective arises that is closer to who make not great decisions, the more you are sincerely interested in getting to know all of those different versions of yourselves, the more you are able to actually choose which version of you, you end up being.

The last thing I wanted to encourage you to do is to remember what I call common humanity. The more that you investigate yourself, the way that your mind works, the more you are learning about other people as well. Sometimes the greatest source of willpower and self control is understanding that we are all in this together, that we all in some way struggle with stress, we all in some way struggle with putting things off and investing in the future, all of us are tempted by something, all of us have emotions that can be difficult to regulate, and this says more about what it means to be human than about you as an individual.

The more we get to know ourselves, the more connected we often feel to other people and the less isolated we feel in our own struggles. In fact, it is this sense of connection to others through our own struggles that turns out to be one of the greatest sources of willpower, that when we know that our own will observe what is happening with a kind of non-judgmental curiosity, who is really interested in understanding how things work, and that includes how you work. You can observe yourself in your own mind as if you were a scientist trying to figure out how does this work.

The more you see, the more you can often influence how that process works. To think about giving yourself willpower experiments, that you can try new ways of thinking, you can try on new ways of acting, and you can just watch to see what the outcomes are. There is almost playfulness that can come into it where rather than always having to know the right way to do something, you can really experiment with yourself and treat your life as an experiment and use different strategies to see what best supports you.

I also encourage people to get to know every aspect of themselves. We started this conversation tonight with the idea that we always have inner conflicts, that there are different versions of you competing for your own time and trying to make the decisions, and it is my experience that the more you understand those different aspects of yourself, including the parts of you

We saw that we can come in and start with our body, that we can do simple things like get more sleep, or exercise, or slow down our breathing, and that changes how we think and the choices that we make. We also saw that you can go to the complete other extreme, and rather than controlling anything that is happening in you, you can think about turning to others for support and strengthening relationships with people you care about in a way that gives you greater willpower and allows you to support them in their challenges as well. We saw that how you think about yourself can have a very big impact on the decisions you make. One way to become the better version of yourself is to get to know the future self that you want to be, that a process of imagination can actually give you more self control and more strength in the present day. All these different types of strategies that you can jump in anywhere in that continuum and begin to strengthen your willpower.

The last thing that I wanted to do was offer the final takeaway points. If you had taken my full Science of Willpower class, the things that I think are really helpful as you go out into the world and you try on different strategies of supporting yourself. One is to think of yourself as a scientist. A scientist is somebody who hold that bigger perspective and recognize that your own mistakes are part of the process of being human, they do not say what is uniquely wrong with you. That is when people are able to reengage and recommit to their goals.

The last aspect of self compassion is to try to talk to yourself or treat yourself as if you were someone you actually care about, which hopefully you are, and to think about how you would talk to a friend who is thinking about giving up on a goal, or a friend who is trying to go through a difficult change and is really struggling, and to think about being that person for yourself instead of sliding into what is much more common often where we will be self critical to ourselves and say things to ourselves that we would never say to a loved one.

To sum up before we go to questions and answers, I shared with you today just five ideas from the Science of Willpower about how we can choose to be a better version of ourselves. I wanted to review the diversity of these strategies so we have a sense of how many different ways there are of working with our challenges.

steps.

First is mindfulness of whatever it is that you are feeling. This is like what the smokers were doing when they were trying to be with their cravings in a more compassionate and accepting way. This idea that you can allow yourself to feel whatever it is you are feeling disappointment, self doubt, regret, that you can hold that experience with a sense of perspective and caring towards yourself without immediately getting sucked into the intensity of that emotion or that experience.

The second act of self compassion is to remember that whatever it is you are experiencing, you are not the only one. Whatever failure you have experienced, whatever it is you did, whatever it is you want that you are feeling so guilty about, that it probably says more about the fact that you are human than about the kind of human you are, that all human beings fail, all human beings experience setbacks, all human beings make mistakes. Most often, when we are experiencing our own stress and difficulties, we forget this. When we forget how human it is to make mistakes, that is when we lose our willpower to reengage with our goals. Studies have shown that when you are able to difficulties with guilt or with shame. This diagram is meant to indicate that your prefrontal cortex, the home of willpower, is no longer able to regulate the areas of the brain that produce stress, anxiety, and cravings, and other impulses.

The very experience of being ashamed of your difficulties or feeling guilty about something that you have done takes away your willpower and it paradoxically makes you more likely to repeat that mistake or more likely to give in to that desire that you feel bad about yourself for having. Self compassion does the exact opposite.

The last thing that I wanted to share with you is the practical strategy for giving yourself self compassion in a difficult experience, whether it is something like temptation or anxiety, or whether it is actually trying to forgive yourself for something you have done where you failed or maybe you have let someone else down, and you are feeling guilty and ashamed about that, and it is starting to feel like it is going to be impossible to repair that relationship or impossible to reach a goal.

This is something that is used in the Science of Self Compassion, having people talk to themselves through three very simple whether it is ordinary food temptations or people who experience actual food addiction and binge eating. It has also been shown to help people who struggle with addiction to alcohol and other substances and even people who struggle with anxiety disorders that people can learn to treat their own fear and anxiety in this friendly and compassionate way where turning your attention to your own stress and suffering takes away the power and gives you back the freedom to make other choices that are consistent with your goals.

Of all the science that I have told you about today, this is the thing that I use most in my everyday life. This idea of not being able to get rid of difficult inner experiences or difficult emotions, but being able to be with them in a way that is like being a friend to myself and then being able to make a different choice based on my goals rather than always acting out of fears or out of temptations and cravings.

This idea again, if you look at what is happening in the brain when one is compassionate towards one self, what you see is that it gives you back your prefrontal cortex. This is an image showing what happens in your brain when you respond to your own

Chapter 5

You can see that the premotor cortex is the area of your brain that plans what you are going to do. Most of the times when a smoker experiences a craving, that part of the brain is literally planning a message to your arm to reach into your pocket or your jacket and pull out the cigarettes and your lighter. When you experience a craving, your brain is already telling your arm what to do. What the researchers found is that being compassionate and mindful towards your cravings and stress turned off that automatic connection so that even though you were experiencing a craving and stress, the brain was no longer automatically responding to it with action.

This is the opposite. Most people's intuition is, oh my gosh, when I experience stress or cravings, I have to ignore it. I have to distract myself from it. I have to escape it. This is suggesting thinking of yourself more as being like a caregiver for your own inner experiences or being a friend to yourself through those difficulties. This technique has been shown to work not just for smokers, but also for people who are struggling with food issues, apply compassionate attitude towards your own cravings and your stress about not being able to give in to them.

In the study, they put people in a brain scanner so they can see what happens in the brain as they try this strategy. As they are in this brain scanner, they see a series of photographs related to smoking which always trigger cravings among people who want to smoke and are also trying to quit. In the study, some of the times, they were using this mindful attitude of acceptance and self compassion towards their craving, whereas other times, when they saw those pictures, they were told not to do that, just to allow yourself to react normally. What the researchers found is that when people paid attention to their own cravings and stress with this mindful and compassionate attitude, it reduced the craving, it reduced the stress. This is what the smokers told them. When you looked at what was happening in the brain, you see reduced activity in areas of the brain that are associated with stress and cravings. More importantly, what they found was that there was a functional disconnection between the stress and cravings areas of the brain and the areas of the brain that usually respond to cravings with action.

What makes this a willpower intervention is that some of those people were taught a strategy for how to deal with their own cravings and with their own stress about not being able to smoke. That strategy was to pay full attention to what it felt like to want the cigarette and how hard it was not to be able to smoke, to feel it in their bodies, and to try to bring a mindful and compassionate awareness to their own suffering in wanting the cigarette.

It turned out that the people who learned the strategy of self-compassion and mindfulness for their own cravings and stress, that even though they were not told to reduce their cigarette-smoking, over the next week, they cut down almost 40% without even really trying. There was something about learning how to be with their own cravings and their own stress that made them better able to act on their goal of quitting smoking. This is just one example of how learning a more compassionate way to be with your own difficulties can strengthen willpower.

This is another study of the same technique. This was also with smokers who wanted to quit but had been unable to quit. This was a study that looked at what happens in the brain when you a smoking study, and they thought they were going to be able to smoke right away.

But instead, the researcher put them in a room and walked them step by step through a torture test. They began by telling them to pick up their pack of cigarettes and hold it their hands. They are thinking, great, I get to smoke now. But instead, this voice comes into the room from an intercom, and the voice says, Stop. Then they have to fill out a form rating how much they want to smoke and how much stress they are feeling about not being able to smoke.

They have to wait 2 minutes. Then the experimenter says, okay, we want you to peel the cellophane off the pack of cigarettes. They are like, okay, great. Now I get to smoke. They peel the cellophane, and then that voice comes in on the intercom and says, Stop. And they fill out the forms again. Then the voice says, okay, we want you to take a cigarette out, and they do that. Stop, we want you to smell the cigarette. Stop, put the cigarette in your mouth. Stop. Pick up the lighter. Stop. That went on for 2 hours. That is why it was a torture test.

for ourselves. That can be an additional source of self control when we recognize that anything we do to benefit ourselves will also be benefiting the people that we care about.

Now we have to talk about a torture test. The last idea that I want to share with you is the idea that in my classes, people are most likely to argue with, it tends to most go against people's intuition about how to strengthen self control. This is the idea that self compassion is a far greater source of self control than self criticism, or guilt, or shame.

In fact guilt, shame, and self criticism steal our self control from us. It does not contribute to it. Forgiving ourselves and accepting our own stress and suffering and even our own weaknesses, make us stronger.

I want to tell you two different ways that that plays out. The first involves a torture test in which people who wanted to quit smoking were asked not to smoke for 12 hours, so they really, really wanted a cigarette. Then they were brought into the laboratory, and they brought with them their favorite pack of cigarettes, and they brought a lighter because they knew this was contributing to my social environment? Both of those ways of thinking helped me expand the sense of what is possible in terms of supporting myself and supporting others.

One of the things that I always encourage people to do is to think about first of all, who in your life is already being a role model for you, for good or bad? Who is contagious in your own life and who are you catching things from? And to look for the people in your life who already share the goals and the values that you want to commit to, to really find the people in your life who will support your goals.

Research shows that even thinking of somebody who shares your goal or supports your goal gives you more willpower when you are feeling the most overwhelmed and most exhausted. It is important to know what those relationships are and to strengthen those relationships as a way of strengthening your own self control.

I also like to think about how the choices that I make might be a positive influence on other people I care about. Sometimes we are willing to do for other people, but we are not so willing to do

We also know that the human brain has a number of brain cells called mirror neurons that are constantly paying attention to what other people are thinking and feeling. This is another way that we can catch willpower or that we can share willpower with others. When you are around other people and you see them giving in to temptation, the brain is automatically trying to understand that person's experience, and the way that the brain does that is it recreates that experience in your own brain.

You have probably had an experience like that with physical pain, or illness, or emotions where you were with someone you care about and they are in pain, or they are very upset, and it feels contagious. Suddenly, you start to flinch as if you were in pain or you begin to become upset as well. That same process seems to happen for goals and for willpower, that when you are around other people who are demonstrating personal strength, you catch it. When you are around other people who are stressed out and out of control, you catch that state.

One of the things that I started to think about a lot is not just to focus on self control, as in how well am I controlling myself, but how well is my social environment controlling me. What am I can see on to the inside of it. You are looking at the area of the brain that I have been talking about as the source of Want power. This is the area of the brain where you hold your deepest goals and your values. Importantly, you know who you are. This is the region of the brain where the sense of self resides. What you are looking at here is wherein the brain becomes more active when you think about yourself. This bottom picture is what becomes active in the brain when you think about your mother.

These are very similar. It is very different when you think about a stranger. In some very important way when you think about the relationships that matters to you, you are thinking about yourself. One of the ways we know who we are is through our relationships and the roles that we play that connect us to other people. That means that other people become part of your own Want power, that when you know other people care about something, it automatically becomes part of your own goals and values. This is one of the ways that we catch willpower or willpower failures, that if someone you care about makes a change, the brain is automatically beginning to incorporate that change and that goal into your own sense of self.

They found a similar pattern for all sorts of willpower behaviors, whether it is related to drinking, spending in debt, even cooperation that when one person makes a decision to behave in a more altruistic and compassionate way, that behavior starts to spread within social networks. This idea that I found very helpful and very important to keep in mind is how contagious our own choices are and how much we are influenced by the people around us.

I started to wonder why is it that willpower is contagious, both the willpower successes and the willpower failures. Again, I got curious about the brain, and I wanted to share with you just two ideas from neuroscience that helps us understand why it is that we are so influenced by other people. One of them is the idea that when we think about who we are, we do not just think about ourselves. Interestingly, our sense of self includes other people, and it particularly includes other people we care about.

What you are looking at here is a brain imaging slide, and these are different types of brain slices. Just to orient you, you have to imagine me standing this way, and a giant blade cuts my head in half. You are going to take off the front half of my head, so you

Chapter 4

The next big idea that took me by surprise was when Harvard researchers first published the idea that willpower is not only about self control. We often think about self control as being us, controlling our own thoughts, our own actions, and our own choices. But it turns out that we are very much influenced by other people.

The Harvard researchers discovered that if a friend of yours gains weight, it dramatically increases your chance of gaining weight in the future. The same is true of a spouse or a family member. They found that you could see obesity rates increasing, and it is spread out through social networks of liking and mutual respect.

Obesity was the first willpower failure that they observed. But they found that it also worked for willpower successes, so that if one person in a social network quits smoking, it increases the chances that his or her friends and family would quit smoking.

avatar get thinner or get stronger. Researchers have found that when you can see the possibility of change in your future self, when that vision is clear and it really feels possible, you will run longer and work harder.

If you put all these studies together in thinking about the future self, it becomes important to think about your future self as someone you care about and also as somebody who is receiving the consequences of the choices that you make today and recognizing that every single choice you make today is creating this future you who may be a very different version of you in both a good way or in a bad way.

Anything that you do, the time that you take to think about with clarity who do you want to be and how it is going to feel in 10 years or 20 years, if you continue to make the choices that you make today, that can be something that can give us a lot of motivation both in terms of investing in our future and also appreciating the great possibility that each of us has for change.

Taking somebody who currently smokes and is interested in quitting but is really struggling to quit and then showing her two possible future selves that this is what you will look like in 10 years if you quit smoking, and this is what you will look like in 10 years if you keep smoking, and asking people to imagine what this person might feel like and what this person might feel like in terms of their energy and their health. Maybe this person has gratitude to your present self for having the strength and the courage to quit smoking to contribute to your future self's health and wellbeing.

In another study that was done at Stanford University, they found that seeing your future self, even if it is like yourself next week, not necessarily in 10 years or 50 years, and that change is possible in your future self in the short-term is also very motivating to help people make difficult choices.

This is a technology where an individual is running on a treadmill. This person will see an avatar of himself running on a treadmill or not running on a treadmill. The person in real life is exercising on a treadmill, and if he slows down, he sees his avatar get fatter. If he starts walking or running faster, he will see his

Then they gave the participants money and asked them, what do you want to do with this money? The young people saved twice as much money for retirement after they had been introduced to their future self than if they had not spent this time with their future self.

In fact, when I first started talking about the study, it seemed like it was an interesting technology, but how would we ever use it. A student of mine just sent me an advertisement today from Merrill Lynch that is using this technology on the web to introduce investors to their future self. You can upload your own photograph, and you can meet your future self, and then they will help you make investments. The idea is that this will help people make good choices about what to do with their money so that their future self is well taken care of.

But it is not just about saving money. It is also about doing things that help contribute to your future self's health and longevity. Another example of an intervention that is using this idea of how important it is to be connected to your future self is doing things like this.

tend to feel like their future self is a total stranger. This was a study that was trying to find out whether you could increase the chance that a young person would be willing to save money for the future if they were introduced to their future self in the retirement age. What you are seeing here is a 3D technology that allows people to see an aged version of themselves, as if they were actually in a room with them, a three-dimensional avatar.

If I were in a study, I would come in, sit down, and I would be looking into these 3D goggles, and I would see a version of myself at age 70. I would be staring right at her. Because this technology uses video cameras to record my facial expressions and my movement, when I say something, I actually see my future self say it. In this particular study, they had young people interview and have a conversation with their future self.

It would be something like me sitting here as my present self saying to my future self, what is your name? Then as my aged future self, I would say back, I am Kelly. My present self would actually see myself answer back. In the study, they had a whole interview, and it was a lovely conversation getting to know your future self.

to your future self. You think of that future self as somebody you have an obligation to take good care of, that you want to make sure that that future you is happy and healthy, but also that you feel like there is some possibility of positive change that who you are now does not necessarily dictate who you will be in the future.

That is a really good place to be psychologically. When you feel caring towards your future self, but also feel a sense of optimism that that change is possible, that is when you are most likely to take on new challenges. That is when you are most likely to invest in your future. There are many interventions now trying to help people find that middle ground where they really feel interested and connected to their future self. Their future self does not feel like a stranger, but also that that future self feels like someone who might be a nicely developed version of your present self.

To give you an example of this, I was told today that here in Japan, you do not have as much of a problem with this as we do in America. This was a study that was done in the United States bringing young people into the laboratory, young people who is 10 or 20 years older than your present self. This survey is asking you to pick a set of circles that best represents how close, connected, and similar to your future self do you feel right now.

Is that person a total stranger? That would be these circles here where your current self feels like a completely different person than your future self. That future self is a stranger. You do not know who that old person is. That is not me. Or maybe if you are a little bit connected to your future self that you can say, yeah, I have a sense of who that person is and what she wants, or what he is going to be experiencing and thinking. All the way down to this set of circles here, people who feel like actually who I am in the future is who I am now. I feel very connected to, very close to, and very similar to my future self. I invite you to think for a moment, where you might place yourself on the spectrum, how close to, connected to, and similar do you feel to say who you will be in 10 or 20 years.

Researchers have found that where you place yourself on this survey can have a very profound impact on the choices you make. Where you might ideally want to be is somewhere in the middle of spectrum where you both feel connected to and close possible step you can think of and be willing to take that very small step, and treat it like a willpower workout. By doing something that is one step harder than what you are used to, it becomes easy. The things we think of as being not like us, the strengths that we think we do not have, maybe other people have it, I could never quit smoking or I could never do that thing that I am terrified of, that actually we acquire that strength in the same way that we acquire physical strength. This is something I also want to remind and encourage you of that if there is something in your own life that you are striving towards, but it seems so far away from what is possible right now, to think about training your brain and training the strength of willpower in the same way that you would train your physical body.

The next idea that I wanted to share with you involves actually something that you can think about yourself for a moment. I want to explain what you are looking at here. This is a survey that some of my colleagues at Stanford developed to help people think about the relationship that they have with their future self. You might imagine your future self 10 years or 20 years in the future, think about who that person is, this future you who

The next idea I wanted to share with you is much simpler. This is the idea that willpower is a trainable skill, and that your brain learns from experience how they get good at whatever you ask it to do. Much like a physical muscle, say your biceps, if you wanted to strengthen your arm, you could do that by giving yourself workouts. You could pick up something heavier than you had ever picked up before, lift it a few times, and by doing so, your muscle is going to learn from that challenge, and it is going to change itself so that it will be easier to lift something heavy again. We know that is how the physical body works. It turns that is also how the brain works. The areas of the brain that are most responsive to learning are the areas of the brain responsible for willpower and self control.

The second idea that changed the way I think about willpower is, I used to think if there was something I wanted to do that was difficult, a habit I wanted to change or a big project that I had to face, I always thought I had to figure it all out beforehand. I had to know how to do it. I had to be able to do it all at once.

This research helped me see that often the best way to make a very big change or to reach a very big goal is to take the smallest became more activated when blood sugar levels went up, and it became less activated as people's blood sugar levels were going down. The area of the brain that became more activated when blood sugar levels went down were areas in the middle of the brain that are associated with the impulsive self, that are associated with cravings, temptations, and stress.

To me, it was very interesting that you could completely transform people's personality and their choices by manipulating something as simple as blood sugar, and that perhaps, we could change in some ways our own personalities and shape our own choices by making decisions about not letting our blood sugar level get too low.

Again, these are all examples of basically, small choices that we make every day that change what is happening in our body that can have a powerful impact on our mind. That was the first idea that I wanted to share with you, thinking about who you are from a biological point of view and thinking about taking care of our body as one of the most important things we can do to be the best version of ourselves.

brought people into the laboratory and hooked them up to IV drips in their arms. They controlled the levels of two substances that were going into their blood stream. They were controlling insulin, which helps us take up blood sugar, and they were also controlling direct glucose, putting sugar into the blood stream. By controlling both insulin and glucose, they could literally manipulate people's blood sugar, moment to moment without you knowing what is happening.

You are just sitting there. You do not know what is going into your arm, and they are lifting your blood sugar up and then they are dropping your blood sugar and boosting it and dropping it. While they are doing this, they are tempting you with things and asking you to make choices while they are controlling your blood sugar. What they found was they could completely change people's decisions based on what they were doing to their blood sugar.

What you are seeing here is a picture of the brain, and again, this is the same type of slice of a brain. The red, yellow, orange, that is the prefrontal cortex. This is the area of the brain that we think of as being the home of willpower. That area of the brain lower, say because they skipped a meal or because they eat a diet that leads to big ups and downs in your blood sugar levels, say eating mostly junk food diet, when people's blood sugar levels are low and not steady, they become the worst version of themselves. They are more likely to be aggressive. They are more likely to rely on stereotypes and act in ways that are biased or prejudiced. They are more likely to give in to temptations. They are more likely to procrastinate.

What is fascinating to me is that researchers have given people snacks or drinks that boost their blood sugar and found that you could reverse people's decisions. People are more likely to invest money in the future after they have had a little boost in their blood sugar levels. They are more likely to volunteer time for charity if they have had a boost in their blood sugar levels. This idea that something as simple as when was the last time you ate, when was it that you had a snack, could influence your ethics and your choices, surprised me.

I wanted to share with you one of the studies that is not in the book. This is a more recent study at Yale University, and I thought this was truly astonishing. This particular study reward or getting a negative outcome. Sometimes becoming a better version of yourself can be as biologically simple as resting the brain.

It also turns out that many things we do that we think of as taking care of our body or helping us deal with stress, turn out to be ways of boosting our willpower reserve. Basically, anything that restores you can be something that also builds willpower. Sometimes we think of them as being self-indulging.

Many of us have very busy lives. We have a lot of obligations with family, a lot of obligations with our careers. It may feel like we do not have time to do things, like exercise, or meditate, or do yoga. But it turns out that these are ways of shifting our biology so that we are more likely to be walking around the world in a state of brain and body that allows us to be that best version of ourselves.

One other aspect of biology that shocked me when I learnt about this research was the observation that even your blood sugar levels can very much shape the decisions that you make. Scientists have found that when people's blood sugar levels are

When I saw that study, I thought we can choose this. We can choose to change what is happening in our bodies by very simple things, like slowing down the breath. One of the first insights that I got from this particular Science of Willpower is how important it is to take care of your body. There are simple things you can do to your body that have a powerful impact on your mind, and doing things like choosing to slow down your breath can allow you to shift out of a stress response and give you willpower when you are facing something that can be a very important challenge.

Chapter 3

It turns out that when people are not getting adequate sleep, the part of your brain where the Want power lives becomes unable to remind you of what your most important goals are. When people have not had adequate sleep, they find temptations more tempting, and they are less able to control their impulses. They become worse at predicting the consequences of their choices. If it were something like say a risky investment, they become less able to see what the risk is and predict the likelihood of getting a like offering people a little bit of money today, 'would you like a small amount of money today or would you be willing to wait 1 week, and I will give you more money?' You can predict whether people will choose the larger reward that they have to wait for, again by whether their heart shifts towards a slower rate and their breathing shifts towards a slower rate, that there is something happening in the brain and the body that is a signature of self control.

One of the studies that I find most poignant took people who were addicted to alcohol and were working very hard not to drink, to stay sober. In this particular study, they took these alcoholics and showed them an alcoholic drink. They looked at whether those alcoholics had a fight-or-flight stress response on seeing the drink or whether they had a pause-and-plan willpower response. Then, they looked at who was likely to relapse over time. They followed them to see who ended up giving in to the addiction and failing to stay sober.

They found that you could predict who was going to relapse by whether or not their bodies shifted into a stress response or a willpower response in the face of this temptation.

room.

They were measuring things like heart rate and breathing, and they found that, people who were able to resist temptation, they shifted into this physical state that they then called pause-and-plan. Later, researchers found that you see the exact same thing happening in the body when people are persevering at a difficult task, even in the face of failure or negative feedback.

For example, one study gave women negative feedback on an intelligence test. They told the women that they performed very, very poorly. But then they told the women, we found that sometimes if you do the test more than once, you can learn from it and improve your performance. Would you like to try again? And you could predict which women would say, 'Okay, I didn't do so well. But I am going to try again and see if I can improve.' You can predict which women were willing to do that again and take on that challenge, by whether or not their body shifted into this pause-and-plan response, whether their heart rate slowed down, and whether their breathing slowed down.

The same has been true for other types of willpower challenges, most important values and goals, it shifts into a very different state, one that slows down your heart rate, slows down your breathing, and actually, sends extra energy to your prefrontal cortex.

It is the exact opposite of the stress response. Now your brain is better able to think about, do I want the consequences of eating all those extra sweets? Or do I want the consequences of resisting temptation? It actually gives you the 'I Won't' power to say 'No'. Or in other circumstances, it would give you the 'I Will' power to do something even in the face of anxiety or stress.

This pause-and-plan response turns out to be, basically, the physical signature of willpower, and not just for things like avoiding temptation. This pause-and-plan response was first identified by researchers who brought people into the laboratory and put a plate full of cookies, brownies, chocolates, and other tempting foods, and then told them, these goodies are for the next participant, you are not allowed to eat them; instead, you are only allowed to eat the carrot sticks and the celery sticks that we have provided for you. Then the researchers left the some of you, this might be scarier than a tiger running into the room if you are somebody who struggles to control your impulses around sweets or foods, or you could imagine any temptation that you might struggle with. When you meet this treat, if you have a fight-or-flight stress response to it, forget about self control, your prefrontal cortex is going to be shutting down. You are going to be acting on automatic habit and impulse, and you are probably going to eat every last cake on that tray.

We need a different way of responding to challenges and threats to our long-term goals. We need a different way to find the types of resources that are going to help us meet this kind of challenge, not the ones that are about life or death in this moment, but that are about making small choices day-to-day that can create wellbeing in the long term.

The good news is we have an instinct that is pretty much the opposite of the fight-or-flight stress response. Scientists call it the 'pause-and-plan' response. When your brain recognizes a threat to your long-term goals, not a threat to your immediate survival, but something that is going to pull you away from your

But one of the interesting things about the fight-or-flight stress response is that in order to help you act on survival instinct, it actually begins to shut down activity in the prefrontal cortex, the area of the brain that has the 'I Will' power, 'I Won't' power, and 'I Want' power. When your body begins to release adrenaline and cortisone, the stress hormones that help you fight or flight, when these hormones circulate back to your brain, they begin to selectively turn off the brain cells that would ordinarily give you willpower and help you think about the big perspective in your life. Makes a lot of sense in a life or death crisis that you do not want to be thinking too much about your options, you want to act now.

But as we will see it, it has a lot of implications on our ability to be our best self when we understand how stress, even psychological stress, without tigers running around the room, but anytime, we feel threatened or uncertain, how that might interfere with our ability to be our best self.

Tigers are not the only challenge that we face. It may be possible that when you leave tonight, you could run into a very different kind of threat to your wellbeing, one that looks like that. For

To understand that willpower is something that happens in your brain and your body is actually very helpful in thinking about the two different ways that the human brain and body respond to challenges.

I want you to imagine for a moment that we are in this auditorium, things are very calm and restful right now. What if all of a sudden, in through these doors, running on to the stage was that. That would be very alarming, yes? Yes. You might start to freak out a little bit because this is not an ordinary occurrence. This guy did not have dinner, and he may be heading down the aisles, looking for dinner. If that actually happened, your body and brain would mount fight-or-flight response, or a stress response. This is an instinct that you have when you recognize threat to your survival. The brain and the body shift into this mode automatically. You might notice your heart pounding. You might notice that you are breathing harder and faster. You might notice that you are sweating a little bit, and you might find it very difficult to focus on anything except for that tiger and where he is headed. All the resources in your brain and body become mobilized to help you deal with this life or death crisis that you are facing. It is very adaptive.

insights from the Science of Willpower. If you have read the book, these are going to be some familiar ideas, and you may hear some studies that you have read about. I hope that it is fun to meet now as friends and think about some of these ideas and hear some of these studies again. These are the things that most surprised me when I began to study not just my intuition about how people can be their best selves, but really what the science says.

I am delighted to be sharing with you the things that I changed my mind about as I learned more about the science, about how the brain works, about the things in our environment, and the way we may think that makes it easier to make difficult changes and be the best version of ourselves.

We are going to begin with the biology of willpower. This is one of the biggest insights from science that completely changed the way I think about who I am and how I make choices. This is the idea that you can think of willpower not as some personality trait that you have or you do not have, not as some moral virtue, but as something that happens in your brain and in your body, that there is a real physiology or physical response of willpower.

to contribute to the world, and what you want to experience in your life?

This turns out to be as much of a strength and skill as the ability to resist temptation. The ability to know what your goals are and to have a clear picture of your life is as much of a skill and strength as those other aspects of willpower that we may be more used to thinking of.

Chapter 2

Tonight's talk is about understanding how can I be a better version of myself. How can I choose to be in that state of mind that has the wisdom and courage to say 'No' to temptation and also say 'Yes' to challenges, and be willing to show up for those challenges. How can I be the version of myself who remembers my deepest values, my most cherished relationships, and my strongest goals, so that when I face distractions and temptations, I am able to choose what matters most.

To do that, I am going to share with you five of my favorite attention on whether it is studying, or exercising, or whatever it is that you might tend to put off because it is difficult, this is the part of the brain that produces the feeling of wanting to do it, the willingness to do things that are difficult, I call that 'I Will' power, that I have the will to take action that will lead to consequences that I want in my life.

The right side of the prefrontal cortex is the part of the brain that does the very important job of resisting temptation. That is the part of your brain that says 'No' when maybe other parts of your body are very interested in saying 'Yes', in giving in to temptation and following your short-term desires. This is what I call 'I Won't' power, the ability to say 'No' when you find yourself being pulled in a direction that is not helpful and may actually be quite destructive.

The last part of willpower, which is the one that is the most elusive for many of us, is the ability to remember what it is you really want when you are walking about in the world and you run into distractions and temptations. You start to experience emotions and stress, that is, do you know who you are and what you want? Do you have a clear vision for life, of what you want remember our values and the things that we hold close to our heart. We also understand ourselves in relationship to other people so that we are able to hold multiple viewpoints about our needs and other people's needs and balance those well.

So, you can imagine that when you are in this state of mind, you are going to make a very different choice when it comes to how you spend your time, and do you give in to temptation, and are you willing to take a risk and do something difficult. You are going to have a very different decision based on whether you are in that part of your mind or the other part of your mind.

When I talk about willpower, what I am talking about are three different strengths that allow us to choose to be that version of ourselves who takes a big picture, who understands long-term goals, and has the strength to do what is difficult that we will be grateful for later on. What you are looking at here is a picture of two different willpowers in the brain. This part of the brain, we have got the prefrontal cortex. We have got the left side of the prefrontal cortex, which is responsible for the ability to do things that are challenging. If you think about what it takes to get out of bed early in the morning and put your energy and different modes of operations that the brain has which produces two totally different versions of yourselves.

When you are in one mode of the brain, you have one type of goal, you have one type of personality, and you are likely to make one type of decision. When you are in the other mode of the brain, you have a completely different personality. You have a different agenda, different goals, and you make different choices. Throughout the day, and throughout our lives, we go back and forth between these two different modes of the brain.

We have a mode of the brain that is very impulsive, that when we are in this system of the brain, we tend to think about what is in our best interest right now. We are interested in immediate gratification. We are interested in avoiding pain. We are only focused on this moment.

But when we are in the other system of the brain, which is sometimes referred to as self control as opposed to the impulsive self, we take a much bigger picture or perspective on our lives. We understand our long-term goals. We tend to be very good at predicting the consequences of things that we do today. We this choice, or are you going to give in to the opposite? This has been something that philosophers and great religions have speculated on for a long time.

As a scientist, I am very interested in how modern psychology and study of the brain can tell us more about this very common human struggle. Why is it that we often feel like we have this inner conflict that gets in the way of being our best self or realizing our goals?

What I want to talk about today is this inner see-saw that many of us experience where we want to be good, but then we find ourselves giving in, and how can we actually stack the deck so that we have a chance of being our better selves.

I want to start with one of the latest insights from neuroscience. This idea of why is it that we have so many inner struggles, this competition between different aspects of ourselves. One of the most compelling ideas to come out of neuroscience in the last decade is the realization that although you only have one literal brain inside your head, the brain is better thought of as being two different brains, that you switch back and forth between future self.

Has anyone heard anything that has resonated with you a little bit? Great, okay. If have not heard anything that has resonated with you, I also want to raise the possibility that there could be something completely different which is your own willpower challenge because when I talk about willpower, what I mean is the ability to make choices that are consistent with your values and your goals even when it is difficult. Or even when you are not sure what the right thing to do is, to have the skillfulness, strength, and perspective to make the choices that later on you will be grateful for rather than regret. It could be anything in your life that requires wisdom, skillfulness, and courage.

One of the things that I found in talking to many different people is the sense that even when you have a strong intention to do something positive or to make a change in your life, it seems like some other part of you shows up to sabotage that goal. No matter how good your intention is, there is some other part of you that has a conflict. Many people tell me that they feel like sometimes they are at war with themselves. It is as if there are two people struggling for control. Are you going to make something that brings up anxiety or self-doubt. Sometimes it takes a lot of self control and willpower to make a decision and to take a step even in the face of worries about how it will work out or uncertainty about whether you are even making the right decision.

Also, keeping emotional balance in the face of everyday stress, conflicts, relationship in the workplace, dealing with a lot of inner experiences, whether it is anger, or sadness, or stress, and wanting to use those emotions in a way that does not create further harm to yourself or others, and struggling to find a way to stay in emotional balance in relationships and in a way that is psychologically healthy for us.

Finally, another challenge that I hear about a lot is the struggle to invest in the future without sacrificing present day happiness. We are often asked to make choices that are based on giving in to immediate happiness that would cause our future happiness, or we want to invest in our future happiness, but it requires giving up something now. Many people that I talk to are struggling with this balance of figuring out how much do I invest in my present self versus how much do I invest in my yourself. You can let me know.

First of all, I hear from many people that they struggle with temptations around food, not just food but other things that they desire. There is an inner struggle about whether or not they should give in to temptation now. Does anyone here ever struggled with something like that? I saw one hand. Glad to know that it is not just Americans.

Also, struggling with how we use our time. We may have important goals that we are trying to work towards. But there are also other ways we could use our time that may seem more interesting and fun in the short-term, but that does not get closer to our long-term goals. Perhaps, you also know what the struggle with how you should spend your time like, whether it is something like this gentleman here who is building a very elaborate bridge out of cards or it is your technology, video games, other things that we spend a lot of time on.

I often hear from people that one of their biggest willpower challenges is taking a leap of deciding to go for something that they do not have total confidence in their ability to succeed,

English Transcript

Chapter 1

Hello. It is a great honor to be here. Thank you so much for coming. This is my first time in Japan, and I have been enjoying it very much. There have been many temptations, so I have been getting to practice using my willpower. I want to thank you very much for coming here. I hope that something I say tonight will be of some value to you.

I wanted to start by a little exercise that I often use when I first talk to people about willpower. Wherever I go around the world, I always ask people, what challenges your willpower? When you think about self control and the things that you struggle with, what stands out to you as a major challenge to your willpower or self control? Something that has struck me is that no matter where I go, what country I am in, or where I am, it seems like many people are reporting the same challenges. This is my first time in Japan, so I thought I would do a little reality testing and ask you if these are the things that you are familiar with and perhaps maybe you struggle with some of this

ケリー・マクゴニガル
(Kelly McGonigal, Ph.D.)
ボストン大学で心理学とマスコミュニケーションを学び、スタンフォード大学で博士号(心理学)を取得。スタンフォード大学の心理学者。専門は健康心理学。心理学、神経科学、医学の最新の研究を応用し、個人の健康や幸せ、成功および人間関係の向上に役立つ実践的な戦略を提供する講義は絶大な人気を博し、スタンフォード大学で最も優秀な教職員に贈られるウォルター・J・ゴアズ賞をはじめ数々の賞を受賞。各種メディアでも広く取り上げられ、フォーブスの「人びとを最もインスパイアする女性20人」に選ばれる。ヨガ、瞑想、統合医療に関する研究をあつかう学術専門誌「インターナショナル・ジャーナル・オブ・ヨガ・セラピー」編集主幹を務める。邦訳書に50万部を超えるベストセラーとなった『スタンフォードの自分を変える教室』(神崎朗子訳、大和書房)などがある。

神崎朗子
(かんざき・あきこ)
翻訳者。上智大学文学部英文学科卒業。外資系生命保険会社の社内翻訳等を経て、第18回DHC翻訳新人賞優秀賞を受賞。訳書に『スタンフォードの自分を変える教室』(大和書房)、『ぼくたちが見た世界——自閉症者によって綴られた物語』(柏書房)などがある。

最高の自分を引き出す法 [DVDブック]
スタンフォードの奇跡の教室 in JAPAN

2013年6月30日　第1刷発行

著　者	ケリー・マクゴニガル
訳　者	神崎朗子
発行者	佐藤　靖
発行所	大和書房 東京都文京区関口1-33-4 電話 03-3203-4511

装　幀	水戸部　功
写　真	市川勝弘
本文印刷	シナノ
カバー印刷	歩プロセス
製本所	ナショナル製本

©2013 AKIKO Kanzaki, Printed in Japan
ISBN978-4-479-79392-2

乱丁・落丁本はお取り替えします
http://www.daiwashobo.co.jp

[大和書房の好評既刊]

スタンフォードの自分を変える教室

The Willpower Instinct
Based on the Wildly Popular Course of Stanford University
Kelly McGonigal

ケリー・マクゴニガル
神崎朗子 訳

一度きりの人生が最高の人生に変わる講義

大教室に殺到した受講生たちの「行動」を次々と激変させた「奇跡の授業」を完全書籍化！世界15ヵ国で刊行「NYタイムス」「タイム」他で絶賛を受けた世界的ベストセラー。

定価（本体1600円＋税）
大和書房

明快な説得力と斬新な語り口と実践的な方法論に
「本当に人生を変える」「生涯で最も重要な一冊」と
絶賛のやまない記録的ベストセラー！

定価1680円
※定価は税込（5％）です。